BOULEZ ON MUSIC TODAY

BOULEZ ON MUSIC TODAY

Pierre Boulez

translated by
Susan Bradshaw and Richard Rodney Bennett

HARVARD UNIVERSITY PRESS
Cambridge, Massachusetts
1971

Printed in Great Britain

These studies were written in Darmstadt for Darmstadt.
I dedicate them to the late Dr Wolfgang Steinecke
as a sign of my esteem and friendship.

CONTENTS

'INTERIOR DUOLOGUE'   *page* 11

GENERAL CONSIDERATIONS   16

MUSICAL TECHNIQUE   35

INDEX   144

7

TRANSLATORS' NOTE

When translating a difficult technical work of this kind, there is always the temptation to simplify—even to paraphrase—the original in order to make it more accessible. But, because Boulez's language, however intricate, is extremely characteristic, it seemed dishonest to attempt to dilute its complexity beyond taking certain liberties with the punctuation and adding footnotes where clarification was judged essential. It has proved hardest of all to make a readable version of the opening 'conversation', in spite of his own suggestion that we should translate it into colloquial English . . .

However daunting this book may at first appear, even to the trained musician, we believe it to be both a vital key to the author's musical personality and an important expression of *Music Today*.

Amongst the many who have encouraged and advised us, we would like to thank: Bill Hopkins, for correcting and improving our draft typescript; Françoise Basch and Raymond Perrot-Minot, for their help in the early stages of translation; lastly, and in particular, Pierre Boulez, for his invaluable assistance and patient cooperation throughout.

SUSAN BRADSHAW
RICHARD RODNEY BENNETT
London, 1970

'INTERIOR DUOLOGUE'

— Any musician proposing to embark on an introspective analysis is always suspect.

— Granted, reflection tends to be regarded in an ethereal light as 'poetical' speculation, a safe position, after all . . .

— . . . and it has the great advantage of thriving on imprecision and contenting itself with a few well-tried formulae. Vulgar technical considerations are not thought worthy of a place in the drawing room. They must remain modestly below stairs, and anyone choosing to stress them will certainly be considered ill-bred.

— In fact, you must admit that certain excesses have come about: sometimes longer than necessary has been spent below stairs; we have been shown electricity bills, gas bills and so on . . . All the invoices[1] have been presented, in quantity, and still the questions are no nearer solution! Besides, who can boast of ever solving them?

— However, it would be unfair of you not to admit that self-analysis is generally objected to, just as much 'du côté de chez Guermantes' . . . where the matrimonial régime of sounds is ordered according to an unalterable social tradition, as 'du côté de chez Swann' . . . where free love between the notes is obligatory. This ultimately suggests a very symptomatic mistrust of the intellect on both sides. Shall I quote Baudelaire?

— He won't stop you.

— Right! Listen: 'I pity those poets who are guided by

[1] *Factures* could also mean (musical) 'constructions'; the double entendre is probably intentional. (Trans.)

11

instinct alone; I believe them to be incomplete . . . Somewhere in every poet there must be a critic.' And again . . .

— Again Baudelaire?

— 'I want to illuminate things with my mind and to project the reflection upon other minds.' Keep on listening!

— Still Baudelaire?

— 'The divine goal is infallibility in poetical creation.' Of course, one can juggle with quotations for ever . . .

— Sometimes so that the loser takes all.

— But in fact, one has the right to value Baudelaire's opinions . . .

— He has 'proved' himself, isn't that it?

— . . . especially when he refuses to confuse poetry with 'intellectual nourishment' and 'drunkenness of the heart'; and when he demands a 'mathematically exact' metaphor . . . Right, let's leave Baudelaire!

— No surety will ever be a justification . . .

— I had not taken him as a surety; I find his literary gifts greater than mine: he expressed the fundamental requirements better than I could ever hope to do.

— Modesty, the cardinal sin!

— Did you expect a personal confession of faith from me? I have to disappoint you.

— Modesty again!

— Do you think of me as the spokesman, the standard-bearer . . . ?

— What a glut of military terms! Are you going to say . . . 'of the *avant-garde*'?

— . . . of a school?

— Many find that school aberrant.

— What? Allow me to make use of another quotation!

— If you really must . . .

— I want to show how cultured I am! Here it is: 'On this subject I would ask him to note that when an opinion is held by several learned men, one should ignore the predictable objections which might seem to destroy it, realising that its supporters have already given such easily found objections their attention, and resolved them, since they continue to think as they do'. Whose ironic and trenchant opinion is that?

— Pure polemics!

— Polemics? That's a rather sweeping statement . . . Pascal scripsit.

— He was talking of science and of 'learned men' . . .

— It would be a curious restriction of Pascal's thought to limit it to this particular case. Are there not a thousand ways of being 'learned'?

— Let's return to the 'school'!

— Impossible!

— Does the word offend you?

— I find it ridiculous. This wish to arrange everything in schools is proof of a shopkeeper's mentality. This display on shelves with labels and prices shows, above all, an abuse of authority, of rights, of confidence, in short, of everything!

— Nonetheless, divergencies of personality will lead you to realise . . .

— Alas! They lead me to realise that the living forces of creation are proceeding *en bloc* in one and the same direction.

— You are outrageously biased!

— True! Passion is necessary if a critic is to be exact. What do the feelings of some rag-and-bone man matter to me? My opinion counts a thousand times more than his; mine is the one which will last.

— In plain words, discussion with you is impossible!

— It is just as impossible for me to believe in this shop where 'tendencies' are indexed to the greater glory of tolerance. I pride myself on being supremely anti-dilettante.

— That's a disconcerting reference!

— Anti-dilettante?

— Don't forget that the 'spare, wizened' gentleman disliked brilliant variations on the theme of 'you are wrong because you do not do as I do' . . .

— Yes, but it's different in my case . . .

— . . . and that he tried 'to discover in works the various impulses that gave them birth, and what they contain of inner life'. He found this 'more interesting than the game of taking them apart like curious watches'.

13

— One must still know how to make watches in order to provide fodder for 'do-it-yourself dismantlers'! Anyway, Monsieur Croche had a gift for ambiguous formulae. What do you think of this, amongst others: 'discipline must be sought in freedom . . .'? If there are two words which seem to be opposites, they are certainly discipline and freedom!

— Monsieur Croche wants to shine, to make paradoxes, to flaunt his free and easy manner.

— I feel you are greatly wronging his memory. All the same, let me say that I do not believe in schools, because I am convinced that a language is a collective heritage whose evolution must be taken over, and that this evolution proceeds in a definite direction; but there can nonetheless be lateral currents, shiftings, ruptures, delays, backwashes . . .

— Stop! You are running adrift in a stream of dangerous words which would easily vindicate me.

— Easily? Come now! For that to happen I should have to be dealing in the currency of those misunderstandings that have been accumulated—consciously or unconsciously—by musical historians. They have abandoned themselves helplessly to hero-worship! The reaction was inevitable; now one can speak only of the 'ineluctable necessity of language' or of the 'unbreakable laws of evolution'. As if historical continuity did not have to be 'revealed' by the exceptional personality!

— Are you so sure that no 'exceptional personality' will arise outside what is implied in the historical situation of a certain period?

— A kind of birth of Athene? Unless you find that of Aphrodite more alluring?

— Control yourself! After your 'revelation' I was expecting tongues of fire by now . . .

— Let's leave mythology aside and agree that it would be hard to find that erratic group—'fallen from some dark disaster'?—which was not 'conditioned' by its milieu, so to speak. Besides, historians and aestheticians can, with just a few strokes of the pen, connect everything with everything, and anything with anything. This kind of subtle reasoning is the basis of innumerable theses. Let's forget the sophists! I will prove to you that this 'conditioning' is not, for me, a taboo. I would almost use this phrase—'the enthusiasm of the milieu spoils an artist for me, for I dread his becoming eventually the mere expression of his milieu'.

— Another quotation?

— Guess!

— Baudelaire perhaps? Baudelaire, the dandy?

— No, Croche, the anti-dilettante! Since we have returned to him, I will repeat his formula: 'discipline must be sought in freedom', and conversely I would affirm that freedom can only be found through discipline!

— Perhaps he wouldn't quite agree with you? Perhaps he would flash his 'slow, unbearable smile' at you?

— Too bad! It would be a pity. But we live some fifty years on . . .

— 'Conditioning', in fact!

— Exactly! The situation is far from similar, and we must react differently: intuition is applied to different objectives. We may have to produce a few gas and electricity bills and to dismantle a few watches . . .

— Is your conscience pricking you? Are you getting dizzy? Ought I to encourage you?

— Encourage me? Not at all! As for dizziness . . . I must admit, the path along the ridge is sometimes so narrow that one can only advance one step at a time. How difficult it is to be at once both free and disciplined!

— Melancholy and self-pity! If you go on like this, you will force me to share even your most extreme opinions. Your scruples increase my own, and I almost regret having taken you for a sectarian . . .

— Don't worry! I am quite sectarian enough not to be frightened of dizziness.

— One kick and you surface again! and my suspicions return!

— What did I tell you: 'Any musician . . .'

GENERAL CONSIDERATIONS

All the most important studies and articles which have appeared during the last ten years or so may be broadly divided into two categories: those which set out a critical balance-sheet of the preceding period in all its different phases and various aspects, according to its creative personalities, general developments and particular discoveries; and those which are concerned with a particular point in present-day developments, the description of a recent work, or the justification of a work in progress. I do not find much significance in those would-be 'historical' surveys of the present situation which resemble both journalism and the distribution of prizes and 'Cartes du Tendre';[1] the 'tactical gossip' on which such accounts depend can neither cover up nor compensate for their weakness of thought and total lack of serious study of the scores themselves. They can only be regarded as the poetry-readings of amateur actors, public confessions with the old Dada fragrance 'O alter Duft aus Märchenzeit', in which would-be radical humour descends to the level of the commercial traveller or the exhibitionist autobiographer; their material is skimpy, their manner dilettante; no circus would book such feeble clowns. At best they are occasionally refreshing—'Coca Cola is good for you!'

The majority of studies of the immediate past are of interest for two reasons: the choice of the subject to be analysed and the analysis itself. I have often pointed out that analysis is only

---

[1] *Cartes du Tendre:* 'maps of the affections'—similar to those Victorian pictures which show the paths leading to heaven and hell by way of a virtuous or a debauched life. (Trans.)

of real interest when it is *active*, and it can only be fruitful in terms of its deductions and consequences for the future.

I must clarify my views at this stage in order to avoid any misunderstanding on the question of the method and function of analysis. We have witnessed an abundant crop of more or less absurd analyses which, under various pretexts—phenomenological, statistical, etc.—have ended in debasement and lamentable caricature. 'Responsible' analyses had almost managed to discredit the object chosen for exhaustive study; more recently this has led to investigations based on statistics and information theory which amount to enumerating or describing the fruit on a tree without reference to the tree itself or to its process of fruit-bearing. We are swamped with vast tables of ridiculous symbols, reflections of a void, timetables of trains which will never leave! The existence of phenomena is noted without any coherent explanation being sought for them; nothing can be deduced from this, other than certain obvious periodicities or irregularities, that is to say the most elementary outline. There is also—though I only mention it as a reminder—a form of paraphrase which consists in the graphic transcription of the notated symbols of a score. This boils down to a summary transposition of results already established with the help of a far better system of symbols; a marked weakening is noticeable between the work and its description. As a means of investigation any course must be rejected which does not give as detailed an account of the structures under examination as does their original notation; this mania for graphics can lead straight to illiteracy. A further confusion arises between the detailing of resultant structures—those obtained by processes of derivation or combination—and the investigation necessary for a proper study of the processes themselves and of all their properties: effects and causes are readily interchanged. An account of such structures can be easily understood if presented clearly and intelligently; but even then we are still a long way from a true analytical method. Inventory and description are, at best, only the first step.

In the better cases we find a 'computation' of musical events, but computation and thought do not arise from the same

17

2

process. What then? Should one seek out the composer's thoughts, the paths that have led him from a general, though doubtless rather vague idea, through the pursuit and application of an adequate method to a final, perfectly planned form? Unless the aim is to study the psychology of the composer-in-action, I do not believe that this type of approach can ever be very productive. There is also the disadvantage, dare I say it, of restricting the work to the limits of the composer's creative imagination—a paralysing restriction, for I feel that it is essential to preserve the potential of the *unknown* that a masterpiece contains. I am convinced that however perceptive the composer, he cannot imagine the consequences, immediate or ultimate, of what he has written, and that his perception is not necessarily more acute than that of the analyst (as I see him). Certain procedures, results and types of invention will become obsolete or else will remain completely personal, even though the composer may have considered them fundamental when he discovered them; observations which later turn out to be of great consequence may have seemed to him negligible or of secondary importance. It is very wrong to confuse the value of a work, or its immediate novelty, with its possible powers of fertilisation.

In conclusion, let us define what may be considered the indispensable constituents of an 'active' analytical method: it must begin with the most minute and exact observation possible of the musical facts confronting us; it is then a question of finding a plan, a law of internal organisation which takes account of these facts with the maximum coherence; finally comes the interpretation of the compositional laws deduced from this special application. All these stages are necessary; one's studies are of merely technical interest if they are not followed through to the highest point—the *interpretation* of the structure; only at this stage can one be sure that the work has been assimilated and understood. It would be a delusion, too, to search only for a guarantee or a justification, both useless in themselves.

Is the composer then only a pretext? Michel Butor, at the end of his essay on Baudelaire, gives a definitive answer to this objection. 'Some people,' he writes, 'may think that, while intending to write about Baudelaire, I have only succeeded in speaking of myself. It would certainly be better to say that it was Baudelaire who spoke of me. *He speaks of you.*' If you question the masters of an earlier period with perseverence and conviction you become the medium of their replies: they speak of you through you.

So it is the evolution of our own thought that we see described, with varying success, in those studies which set out, above all, to examine the recent past. It is obvious that Webern —who emerged very early on as the chief landmark in defining our own personalities—stands at the centre of these 'explorations'. There are innumerable commentaries on Webern, but they are only useful inasmuch as they have isolated the lines of force active at the present time: the consideration of the series as a hierarchic distribution, the importance of the interval and of intervallic proportions, the role of chromaticism and of complementary sounds, and the assembling of structures from the different characteristics of the sound phenomenon.

Naturally, in this first category of studies there is a marked tendency to 'generalise', for it is relatively easy to situate a special case in its historical context; in describing present developments, on the other hand, the fact that a general survey of the gradual evolution of language and thought was just as important as a detailed discussion of various morphological and syntactic discoveries has certainly been underestimated. In our 'day-to-day' creative experience, it is certainly difficult, if not sometimes impossible, to stand back from our own immediate preoccupations and, with the necessary objectivity, to make a shrewd, lucid and uncompromising critique of our current achievements.

Deep in the creation of a work, the composer undoubtedly forges for himself a psychology of short-term infallibility. Without this provisory compass—'I am absolutely right'—he would hesitate to venture into virgin territory. This is a sane reflex, which allows him to reach the end of the unpredictable periplus which lies between him and the completion of his work.

Nevertheless, he must be able to judge the distance he has covered along the way, to keep track of his co-ordinates, in short, to make sure that he does not stray from his path. I would not suggest that the final result should be exactly identical with the initial intention—what begins as a portrait may end up as a still-life. (Henry Miller gives a brilliant description of the genesis of a masterpiece in the story 'The Angel is my Water Mark!' from *Black Spring*. I would at least like to quote this passage: 'You may say it's just an accident, this masterpiece, and so it is! But then, so is the 23rd Psalm. Every birth is miraculous—and inspired. What appears now before my eyes is the result of innumerable mistakes, withdrawals, erasures, hesitations; it is also the result of certitude ... The world of real and counterfeit is behind us. Out of the tangible we have invented the intangible.' It is important to make sure that all the forks, twists and turns are integrated into the context: the momentary adoption of a result cannot be justified simply by its immediacy or by well chosen placing. On the contrary the result may obscure the true solution or break the internal cohesion, undoing the logic of co-ordination by refusing to be integrated with the whole. There is sometimes a deep-rooted antinomy between global and partial structures; even though the latter may have been 'foreseen' as subordinates of the former, they acquire, through their own particular lay-out, an autonomy of existence, a true centrifugal force. This phenomenon will be discussed more thoroughly when we go further into the question of form. This may happen in the case of reflections on the different fields of present-day evolution if the results obtained in one field are not verified by researches carried out in the others.

From this point of view, contemporary music, even if it has completely resolved the problem of its paternity, is still far from reaching a general synthesis: year by year, one is hypnotised by such and such a problem or special case. To all intents and purposes one can 'date' many scores—epigonal certainly—according to the character of the preoccupations to which they submit, the temptations to which they yield and the frenzies by which they are possessed; it seems that nothing more than a collective wave has brought on these various fixations. These are dreadful and regular epidemics: there was the year of numbered series, that of novel tone colours, that of co-ordinated tempi; there was the stereophonic year, the 'action' year, the 'chance' year; the 'formless' year is already in sight, the word will spread like wildfire. Let no-one suspect me of over-facile polemics, for proofs abound, as do slavish and minor talents; for this reason I will go no further but will simply state that all collectivity, especially when it is restricted, as with a collectivity of composers, generates changing fetishes: numbers, large numbers,[1] space, paper, graphics (and graffiti too), of (non)-psychology, information theory, action—and, as a result reaction!—of 'perhaps' and 'why not' and 'what if' . . .

The mentality of such an epigonal group may well be compared to that of primitive tribes; the same reactions to the chosen fetishes. It is said of certain African tribes that if the adopted idol has not performed the services expected of it, it is beaten, mutilated and finally cast out, spat upon and abused, before another, presumed more beneficial, is found. The tribe of epigones behaves no differently: they hurl themselves greedily on a chosen method, obviously having no notion of either its origin or its suitability since they isolate it from all guiding logical thought; they use it according to standard models and having exhausted its more obvious charms, incapable of grasping its internal rigour, they must find a new oxygen supply at all costs: the ant-heap waits for the shock which will galvanise it into moving house again. Such a practice, to put it crudely, suggests a brothel of ideas, and can hardly be considered composition.

The free currency of these fetishes has certainly been useful in clarifying the situation, and this is not a paradox. A period like our own, with all its means of diffusion, has seen them spread very swiftly, but 'epigonism' is not really a particularly remarkable novelty; it is even a necessary evil: it conveniently draws attention to the decrepitude of certain procedures, the non-validity of certain ways of thought—a demonstration *ab absurdo*—and it keeps one's creative conscience alert

[1] The 'law of large numbers': see p. 25.

21

and on guard against being dazzled by novelty, or caught in the narcissistic trap of the mirrors which it creates. 'Epigonism' can perhaps be considered as the sharpest form of criticism, although—or because—it is involuntary. While profiting from the lessons which can be drawn from it, it would be wrong to resent it. Besides, the creative world can always profit from the products of epigonism, even though they have been arrived at in a negative way. Nevertheless, in all honesty I must assert that all these various fetishes arise from a profound lack of intellectualism. This statement will sound strange, for contemporary music is usually judged to be hyper-intellectual. On the contrary, a definite mental regression, in many guises, can be ascertained; this is something I am far from condoning. The power of shock is quickly exhausted; the sensation is dulled, the sparkle vanishes leaving a definite feeling of having been cheated. The summary use of stereophony borders on the delights of cinerama, that is to say, it relies on a cheap and anecdotal idea of space. Space is not the same as the speedway of sound to which it tends to be reduced; space is rather the potential of polyphonic lay-out, an indication of the distribution of structures. The error probably arises from the fact that movement is confused with means of 'transport'. When noise is used without any kind of hierarchic plan, this also leads, even involuntarily, to the 'anecdotal', because of its reference to reality. What was said earlier about the relationship of principal and secondary structures[1] applies exactly to the case of noise and its associations with reality. Any sound which has too evident an affinity with the noises of everyday life (for instance, the most typical: machines and motors—an unexpected piece of luck for those so shrewd as to confuse 'modernism' in musical thought with the 'automation' of contemporary civilisation), any sound of this kind, with its anecdotal connotations, becomes completely isolated from its context; it could never be integrated, since the hierarchy of composition demands materials supple enough to be bent to its own ends, and neutral enough for the appearance of their characteristics to be adapted to each new function which organises them. Any allusive

[1] See p. 20, 'global and partial structures'. (Trans.)

22

element breaks up the dialectic of form and morphology and its unyielding incompatibility makes the relating of partial to global structures a problematical task.

Of all this, the anecdote seems to me the most crucial point. The lesson of the surrealists, in reverse, does not yet seem to have been fully understood.

'The simplest surrealist act,' wrote André Breton in the *Second Manifeste du Surréalisme* (1930), 'consists of going out into the street, a revolver in each hand, and shooting, as randomly as possible, into the crowd.' But he adds this note, 'I am more anxious to know if violence is inborn, before wondering if violence is or is not an act of *composition*.' And later in the same note, 'When I call it the simplest act I am clearly not recommending it above all others because it is simple, and to disagree with me on this matter is like narrow-mindedly asking every non-conformist why he does not commit suicide.' This attitude has hardly changed in thirty years; one frets and fusses around until one comes up against the essential questions which are then dismissed as objectionable: we should be satisfied with the answer 'narrow-mindedly'—it is feeble enough! So we shall never experience the most elementary concert of all, 'shooting as randomly as possible' into the audience, confronting them with the supreme noise—this concert has not yet taken place, perhaps because of a simple misunderstanding between actor and spectator; instead, helpless instruments are maltreated. What meagre compensation it is to hear the last confessions of sadistically tortured piano-lids, the aeolian groans of harps being briskly flogged! In place of the absolute, fundamental act, we have to make do with titillating anecdotes.

History stammers and babbles, as we will see: 'We love neither art nor artists' (Vaché, 1918); 'No more painters, writers, musicians, sculptors, religions, republicans, royalists, imperialists, anarchists, socialists, bolshevists, politicians, proletarians, democrats, bourgeois, aristocrats, armies, police, fatherlands. Enough of these stupidities, no more, no more, nothing, NOTHING, NOTHING, NOTHING' (Aragon, 1920). But by 1928, in his *Traité du Style*, the same Aragon had already

23

replied: 'Thus everyone began to think that nothing is worth the trouble, that two and two do not necessarily make four, that art is of no importance, that being a writer is pretty sordid, that silence is golden. Banalities which from now on will be worn instead of flowers around one's hat' . . . 'There isn't a dirty little *petit bourgeois* still snivelling in his mother's skirt who doesn't set himself up to like idiotic paintings' . . . 'Kill yourself or don't kill yourself. But don't drag your slug-trail of agony, your premature carcass, around the world, stop letting your revolver butt stick out of your pocket inviting an inevitable kick in the pants.' A lot more fun could be derived from this little game of quotations; briefly, a simple rearrangement of certain words would enable these phrases to apply perfectly to certain excrescences and rotting growths of today. Musicians have always been in the rearguard of the revolutions of others; in music, Dadaism still retains the prestige (and naivety) which it has long since lost everywhere else; its flimsy veils hide the sweet sickness of rosy dilettantism. We have learnt from Nietzsche that God is dead, then from Dadaism that Art is dead; there is no longer any need to return to the flood, and to do a reckless revision course on the brilliant demonstrations of yesteryear. We should need the toothpick of Jarry to clean out that miniature stable.

Perhaps I am painting the situation just a little too black? It does seem to me that choice of action, decision in the face of a multitude of possibilities, has become more and more confused with a licentious attitude toward the musical material; libertinage is not liberty, and it often leads to monotony. This mental deviation can easily be analysed, and is accounted for by simple devaluation of the basic concept; starting from the absolute rigidity of the basic plan, at first a margin of error was allowed, a purely material obstruction on the road to perfection; then a coefficient of unforeseen error was admitted, which, shortly afterwards, was required to be unforeseeable. The process became increasingly infectious, and the plan itself was finally found to be corrupt: it too ended up by being intrinsically unforeseen—truly a game of cards without faces and without rules, like Lichtenberg's famous 'blade-less knife

24

with the handle missing'. An accidental gesture in a random construction cannot be very promising architecturally.

It is very easy to see how the situation has developed in just this way. When the serial principle was first applied to all the components of sound, we were thrown bodily, or rather headlong, into a cauldron of figures, recklessly mixing mathematics and elementary arithmetic; the theory of permutations used in serial music is not a very complex scientific concept; one need only reread Pascal to be convinced of this, and to realise that our systems and calculations are summed up in quite modest theories, whose scope is limited to a definite object. Moreover, by dint of 'preorganisation' and 'precontrol' of the material, total absurdity was let loose; numerous distribution-tables necessitated almost as many correction-tables, and hence a *ballistics* of notes; to produce valid results, everything had to be rectified! In fact the basic 'magic squares' were related to an ideal material ('My overcoat also became an ideal'—Rimbaud: *Ma Bohème*), without any thought of contingencies—donkey work—of any kind: rhythmic organisation disregarded realisable metric relationships, structures of timbres scorned the registers and dynamics of instruments, dynamic principles paid no heed to balance, groups of pitches were unrelated to harmonic considerations or to the limits of tessitura. Each system, carefully worked out in its own terms, could only cohabit with the others through a miraculous coincidence. The works of this period also show an extreme inflexibility in all their aspects; elements in the 'magic squares' which the composer, with his magic wand, forgot at the birth of the work, react violently against the foreign and hostile order forced upon them; they get their own revenge: the work does not achieve any conclusively coherent organisation; it sounds bad and its aggressiveness is not always intentional.

Enslaved in such a yoke it was difficult not to feel oneself at the mercy of the law of large numbers: in the last resort, any choice had only a relative importance, simply amounting to cutting a slice of chance. This procedure might be seen as a take-over by numbers; the composer fled from his own responsibility, relying on a numerical organisation which was quite incapable of choice and decision; at the same time he felt bullied by such an organisation in that it forced him to depend on a crippling absurdity.

What could be the reaction to this extreme situation? There were exactly two possibilities: either to break out of the system by expecting no more of numbers than what they could give—that is to say, very little—or to avoid the difficulties by debauchery, seeking justification in what were, after all, pretty banal psychological and parapsychological considerations. The second way was obviously the more tempting, for it demanded only a minimum of effort and imagination.

Dilettantism was thus justified under a new pretext, by renewing a kind of pact or contract with mental laziness and intellectual inconsistency. The most degenerate myths of cheap romanticism were once more flung together, and in effect the primacy of fantasy and inspiration was re-established; the happening, the revelation—absorbing, engulfing—carried all before them. A strange paradox, for this blossoming of 'liberty' conceals the same ideology as that of the most scornful critics of contemporary expression! Even that sacred monster, the interpreter, surfaced and blossomed again in his Pythian role of interpreting the dark designs of the gods of Parnassus (one dares not say of Olympus). Oracles, oracles! Hands and paint-brushes ... I design, thou divinest ... we imagine ... (a resumé of this sparkling poetic art).

At the first opportunity there was a break-out from the stifling prison of *number*, and then EVERYTHING was allowed including the most idiotic and vulgar exhibitionism. Did anyone expect thus to escape the only reality? And what did this general permissiveness and these long holidays from thought signify, if not a continued flight from responsibility? The previous reliance on one aspect of the law of large numbers was now placed on another aspect of this same law. What change was there other than the obvious? The mental process was similar, even if it followed a diametrically opposite direction. On the contrary, one's intellectual equipment should be firmly taken in hand if it is to be controlled and eventually made to create a new logic of sound-relationships. Speculation *itself* must be pitted against a mass of speculations.

Partial speculations are of course indispensable ingredients of a final solution. Sometimes the difficulties to be overcome and the problems to be resolved must be very narrowly circumscribed. There is a terribly pressing and immediate reality, which can only be reached by approaching it from a very definite viewpoint; for composition, in the true sense of the word, brings us face to face with special cases to which tradition —recent as well as ancient—cannot give us the smallest clue, leaving us totally unequipped to cope with them; in these cases there are not only questions of morphology but also problems of structure and of large-scale form. New ways of dealing with material lead us far from traditional solutions. 'Harmonic' functions for example can no longer be thought of as permanent; the phenomena of tension and relaxation are not established on at all the same footing as before, and, certainly not in fixed and mandatory terms; tessitura, in particular, is a deciding factor here. Vertical relationships can be conceived as basic material, as an intermediary factor in the elaboration of complex objects, or as a control in working with complex objects. The vertical dimension cannot be treated identically in all three cases, since each demands special treatment, according to the laws of organisation, which are derived, of course, from a basic but organically specific law. Similarly, horizontal functions have few direct links with the old contrapuntal laws; the regulation of vertical encounters does not observe the same relationships, and the responsibility of one sound in relation to another is established according to conventions of distribution and lay-out. As with vertical relationships, they can be divided into three groups; from point to point, from a group of points to another group of points, and finally the relationships between groups of groups. Figuration itself, in view of the principle of variation, can no longer be generated by the classical canonic formulae; the strict interdependence of these figures obeys other criteria of transformation, according to a very elaborate dissymmetry. From now on the two dimensions of classical (horizontal and vertical) polyphony are

27

linked by a kind of diagonal dimension, whose characteristics figure in each of them, in varying degrees. Independently of any dimension, intervals are developed among themselves in a context whose coherence is assured by complementary chromatic principles. ('Chromatic' is used here in its widest sense, not limited to semitones alone.) The laws which organise structures of duration have absolutely no connection with classical metre, except that they may be based on an equally 'pulsed' time, to give a simple example. Time, like pitch, has three dimensions: horizontal, vertical and diagonal; distribution proceeds similarly by points, groups and groups of groups; these organisations do not necessarily run parallel with those of pitch; finally, time acts as a link between the different dimensions relative to pitch, since the vertical is only the zero time of the horizontal, a progression from the successive to the simultaneous. Because of this morphology, local and global structures—responsible for the form—no longer obey permanent laws. There is also an absolutely new way of conceiving large forms: homogeneity or otherwise of their different components, causality or isolation of their various events, fixity or relativity in the order of succession and in the hierarchy of classification, potentiality or actuality of the formal relationships ... This almost unexplored aspect of form will be examined in detail when we come to deal with this subject.

Partial speculations on all these subjects were necessary and justified; without them none of the different levels of the sound-organism could have been usefully developed. They lead directly to the general speculation which must follow if we are not to remain in the department of seasonal 'novelties'. I would still emphasise that the partial speculations of true creative minds are fundamentally different from the 'speculations' (in the financial sense of the word) of the epigones; the latter could not be integrated with anything at all, because they are comparable to magic 'tricks' for exorcising the essential questions and evading the real answers; to my mind they are of no account in the evolution and formation of contemporary musical thought, depending at the very most on the 'pata-logical'.[1] However, partial speculations, when applied to musical reality, must not veer towards absurdity, by taking the dangerous path of sophism. Nothing is more deceptive or more false than a hasty or misjudged deduction, in spite of its apparent clarity often achieved by a succession of syllogisms that can easily be reduced to over-familiar prototypes: such conscientiously organised aberration is of truly superb imbecility. To retain their validity, speculations must be integrated into a *systematic whole;* then they justify themselves by contributing to this theoretical edifice and of themselves point the way to general principles, the real target of all speculation. It is now essential to forge ahead with this coherent system; it will give impetus to the future development of musical thought and alert it to deviations and to useless, cramping hypertrophies. The weakness of certain recent tendencies of thought is exactly this, that partial speculations have never been fully evolved, hence certain persistent and invalidating contradictions. These must be overcome in order to put contemporary musical thought on a completely and infallibly valid basis.

The word 'logical', used above, leads me to make some comparisons. When one studies contemporary mathematical or scientific thought concerning new structures (of logic, mathematics or theoretical physics) it is clear that an immense distance must still be covered before musicians can reach the cohesion of a general synthesis. Besides, our empirical methods do not in any way encourage the necessary collective effort.

In the field of music, a drastic revision of certain attitudes and a basic reconsideration of problems is essential if the necessary conclusions are to be reached; we must not be

[1] 'Pata-logical': a reference to the cult of ' 'pataphysics', founded by Alfred Jarry. No. 13 of the *Evergreen Review* is a comprehensive introduction to the movement, and from it the following excerpts are taken: ' 'Pataphysics . . . is the science of that which is superinduced upon metaphysics, whether within or beyond the latter's limitations, extending as far beyond metaphysics as the latter extends beyond physics.' And, perhaps more relevant to Boulez's usage: ' 'Pataphysics will examine the laws which govern exceptions, and will explain the universe supplementary to this one.' (From Jarry, *Exploits and Opinions of Dr. Faustroll, Pataphysician.*) (Trans.)

hypnotised by such and such a special case, anecdote or event, for this is to run the greatest risk of reaching an inverse hierarchy between a basic system and its deductions, results and consequences. Take a current example (we will deal with some others in the course of the following chapters): if *at the start* one settles on a plan of immediate action, of instantaneous reaction, of stimulated impulse (a kind of 'automatic writing' of actions and their function, set in motion to order by exact but unforeseen information) this empirically adopted idea is immediately falsified; one should find a system which will inevitably engender these 'provocations' and stimuli rather than writing them according to a fixed disposition whose surface logic can never assume a generative function so as to *organise* the action. Ordering (in both senses of the word) the course of a certain group of events—methodically, empirically or by the intervention of chance—is not at all the same as giving them the coherence of a form. In this connection, I could do no better than to quote these sentences by Louis Rougier on axiomatic method, which could serve as an epigraph to this series of studies: 'Axiomatic method allows the construction of purely formal theories which are both networks of relationships and tables of the deductions which have been made. Hence, a single form may apply to diverse material, to groups of differing objects, provided only that these objects respect the same relationships among themselves as those present among the undefined symbols of the theory.' I feel that such a statement is fundamental to contemporary musical thought; note especially the last clause.

This, then is the fundamental question: the founding of musical systems upon exclusively musical criteria, rather than proceeding from numerical, graphic or psycho-physiological symbols to a musical codification (a kind of transcription) that has not the slightest concept in common with them. The geometrician, Pasch, writes: 'If geometry is to become a deductive science, its procedures of reasoning must be independent of the meaning of geometric concepts just as they are independent of diagrams; nothing but the relationships imposed upon these ideas by postulates and definitions should figure in deduction.'

It is important to choose a certain number of *basic concepts* having a direct relationship with the phenomenon of sound, and with that alone, and then to state postulates which must appear as simple logical relationships between these concepts, independent of the meaning attributed to them. Having established this, it must be added that this condition of *basic concepts* is not restrictive, for, as Rougier says: 'there is a limitless number of equivalent systems of concepts and propositions which can be used as starting points, without any one of them *imposing itself by natural right*'. 'Thus,' he continues, 'reasoning must always be independent of the object involved.' The dangers which threaten us are clearly stated: in relying almost entirely on the 'concrete, empirical or intuitive meaning' of the concepts used as starting-points, we may be led into fundamental errors of conception. Choosing the basic ideas in terms of their own specifications and logical relationships seems to be the first reform urgently needed in the present disorder.

To the objection that to start from the concrete phenomenon is to obey nature and its laws I would answer by quoting once more from Rougier that 'we call "laws of nature" those formulae which symbolise the routines resulting from experience'. He then adds: 'It is a purely anthropomorphic language, for the regularity and simplicity of these laws are only true in the initial evaluation, and frequently the laws degenerate and disappear on further examination.' Léon Brillouin goes further in stressing this: 'It amounts to a confidence trick to speak of the *laws of nature* as if they existed independently of man. Nature is much too abundant for our minds to be able to embrace it. We isolate fragments, observe them, and devise representative *models* (simple enough to be useful)'; he recalls 'the essential role of *human imagination* in the invention'—*not* the discovery —'and the formulation' of these celebrated laws. As much as to say, returning to our own field, that the era of Rameau and his 'natural' principles is finally over; yet that does not mean that we should cease to seek and devise.the *representative models* of which Brillouin speaks.

Before beginning a detailed study of present-day musical thought, it is as well to remember the principles of logic which must be respected, if not of the misunderstandings which are current and abundant. One among many other recent examples is the confusion between pure chance and relativity in the world of sounds and forms, whereas these two concepts, far from coinciding, at no time obey the same structural laws.

This key-word, structure, leads us to a conclusion, again drawn from Rougier, which can equally well be applied to music: 'What we can know of the world is its structure, not its essence. We think of it in terms of relationships and functions, not of substances and accidents.' Similarly we should not start with the 'substances and accidents' of music but rather think about it 'in terms of relationships and functions'.

I fear that after this statement I will be accused of 'pure abstraction' and of forgetting, while speaking of structure, the actual musical content of the work concerned. Here too is a misconception which must be corrected. As the sociologist Lévi-Strauss affirms, on the subject of language proper, I am convinced that in music there is no opposition between form and content, between abstract on the one hand and concrete on the other. Form and content are of the same nature, subject to the same analytical jurisdiction. 'The content', Lévi-Strauss explains, 'draws its reality from its structure, and what we call form is the *structural disposition* of local structures,[1] in other words of the content.' Also these structures must comply with the principles expounded above, concerning the logic of musical form.

In conclusion I wish to stress that the remainder of this book will no longer deliberately adopt a polemical tone, which in the circumstances would be misplaced. Certain paragraphs of this introduction will doubtless seem harsh; there will very likely be much indignation over the anonymity of the allusions: let's have the names! Names? Jesus or Barabbas? This is a question which I shall leave unanswered, like a mirror held up, on

---

[1] It must be clearly remembered that the word *structural disposition* is not meant to suggest a simple summation of these local structures. 'A form', as Paul Guillaume states, 'is something *other* or *greater* than the sum of its parts'.

purpose, before those whose naivety and conceit blend nicely with their amateurism and 'arrivisme'. May they be swallowed up in the contemplation of their own reflection. I will not, however, play at these little war-games; I should not dream of dabbling in 'party politics', with its groups, subgroups, counter-groups and minigroups. I have already spoken of the sociology of epigones and of their behaviour with regard to fetishes; it would be equally interesting to describe their strategy, primitive or advanced, veiled or aggressive; it is a veritable parliamentary birdcage of political parrots in which everybody wants to be more left-wing than his neighbour. Various kernels of a greater or lesser density and influence are formed, each with its own 'inside information', its own vocabulary of command, its parodies of preference, its passwords and accepted ideas. These often end in petty attacks and questions of personality. There is no escape from the welter of 'historical' perspectives (which are intended as milestones but turn out to be Hell's paving-stones), manifestos, miniature dicta (whose flabby paradoxes badly need corseting) . . . Misconceptions can be amusing but it must be realised that we are not fooled by them.

This parenthesis being henceforth finally closed, it is easier for me to say how much respect I have for those, and those alone, who have, with all the powers of invention at their command, contributed to the development of contemporary music. I still will not give names: they are rare enough to be well known. I must stress how much these studies, and my own researches no less, owe to the observation of their work.

Even if I have cause to bring a critical judgement to bear on some details of this true creative activity, my constructive intention should not be ignored: a new universe cannot be discovered without accidents and errors. It seems to me essential to explain the absolute necessity for a logically organised *consciousness*, which avoids slipping into the anecdotal; in concentrating on the anecdote, the most essential problems are completely lost sight of, or seriously misunderstood. Again, I have not touched upon what might be called certain 'meta-logical' categories, such as style (and taste), the specificity

33

of action, not to mention other phenomena which give a musical work its definitive profile.

In the course of these essays I shall try to proceed on the most rigorous level possible—an attempt which will, I hope, allow us all, and myself first and foremost, the better to define present-day musical thought. I feel that this is the most urgent work to be undertaken at present, for discoveries and ideas have followed one another with little cohesion. Let us discipline our mental universe, so that we have no disavowals to face, disillusions to undergo, or disappointments to overcome; let us organise our musical thought strictly: it will free us from the casual and the transitory. Is this not the main discipline with which to resist temptations as futile as they may be seductive? No rushing forward, please—one of the most notorious signs of defeat. Debussy said, penetrate to the naked flesh of emotion; I say: penetrate to the naked flesh of evidence.

MUSICAL TECHNIQUE

A discussion of musical technique in general terms is an ambitious enough project: a thorough examination of this subject in the course of a single small book is almost foolhardy. I do not intend to cover all the questions posed by the present evolution of language, above all since this evolution is taking place at such speed; however, I would like to give a fairly complete survey, and to try to clarify the present state of research, without forecasting future developments. All the same, I am ambitious enough to adopt a general and fairly exhaustive point of view; and I shall start my investigations with reference to certain fundamental ideas.

The world of music today is a *relative* world, that is to say, one where structural relationships are not defined once and for all according to absolute criteria, but are organised instead according to varying schemata.

This world has arisen from the expansion of the idea of the series; this is why I should first like to establish a definition of the series from the strictest point of view, and then to infer from it an ensemble, a network of probabilities. What is the series? The series is—in very general terms—the germ of a developing hierarchy based on certain psycho-physiological acoustical properties, and endowed with a greater or lesser selectivity, with a view to organising a FINITE ensemble of creative possibilities connected by predominant affinities, in relation to a given character; this ensemble of possibilities is deduced from an initial series by a FUNCTIONAL generative process (not simply the consecutive exposition of a certain number of objects, permutated according to restrictive numerical data). Consequently, all that is needed to set up this hierarchy is a necessary and sufficient premise which will ensure the total cohesion of the whole and the relationships between its successive parts. This premise is necessary, because the ensemble of possibilities is *finite* when it observes a controlled hierarchy; it is sufficient since it excludes *all* other possibilities. If the hierarchisation of one of the given aspects of the sound-entity is determined by this necessary and sufficient premise, the other phenomena are free to *integrate* themselves or, simply, to *co-exist* with it; in other words the principle is one of interaction or of interdependence of the various sound-components. (Acoustic phenomena are organic examples of this principle: a sound—generally defined—is, in fact, a sum of frequencies observing in their relationships proportions —variable or not—that are fixed in quality and number, and have a coefficient of dynamics—variable or not. Frequency being in itself a function of time (cycles per second), the sum of the frequencies is subject to a collective dynamic envelope, also a function of time. Thus, from the very first, the complete sound-entity is the result of the interaction of vibration, time and amplitude.) This interaction or interdependence does not function by means of arithmetical addition, but as a vectorial compound, each vector having, from the nature of its material, its own structural properties. Thus there can be either a principal (or primordial) organisation, with secondary (or supplementary) organisations, or a global organisation which takes account of the various categories. Between these two extremes are the various levels of predominance of certain organisations in relation to others, in other words, a dialectic with a vast field of action between liberty and obligation (between free and strict writing).

This idea can be applied to all the components of crude sound: pitch, duration, dynamics and timbre; it applies equally to all the derivatives of these four fundamental ideas: these include both *homogeneous* complexes of pitch, duration, dynamics and timbre, and also *combined* complexes of pitch/duration, pitch/dynamics, etc. In this respect, once again, it seems to me essential to think of the interchangeability of the sound-components as a basic structural phenomenon: at the same time, it should be stressed that they can be graded according to a scale of decreasing importance. In this case, it would be wrong to use the word hierarchy which implies a measure of subordination, since these phenomena are in fact independent, if not in their existence, at least in their evolution: they obey a common principle of structural organisation, even though their evolution shows divergencies born of their own individual characters. Pitch and duration seem to me to form the basis of a compositional dialectic, while intensity and timbre belong to secondary categories. The history of universal musical practice bears witness to this scale of decreasing importance, as is confirmed by the different stages of notational development. Systems of notating both pitch and rhythm always appear highly developed and coherent, while it is often difficult to find codified theories for dynamics or timbre, which are mostly left to pragmatism or ethics (hence the numerous taboos concerning the use of certain instruments or of the voice). Western Europe provides its own eloquent proof of this: the aim of neums was to transcribe pitch more precisely; subsequently, proportional notation was the means of accounting for precise differences of rhythmic values; still later came the need for an adequate transcription of dynamics—it is only since the beginning of the nineteenth century that dynamic indications have become so numerous; at about the same time, specificity and irreplaceability first emerged as real characteristics of instrumentation.

This distinction is not established according to an 'affective' standard, but according to the strength of integration or coordination. Compare, for example, a succession of diverse timbres upon the same pitch and, conversely, a succession of diverse pitches linked by a single timbre, that is to say, interchange the two organisations so as to reverse their specific characters: uniquity and multiplicity. The first case will give the impression of a kind of *analysis* of one component by another, of pitch by timbre; in the second case, the timbre will certainly not appear to be thus *analysed* by the succession of different pitches, since the homogeneity of timbre will impose itself

37

beyond certain internal fluctuations. The uniquity of pitch *integrates* the multiplicity of timbres; the uniquity of timbre *coordinates* the multiplicity of pitches.

For each component, whatever it may be, we will try to establish a network of possibilities which are divisible into the four following categories of value and density, grouped in pairs.

1. *Absolute value* within a defining interval, or module; each value will occur only once, within this module, a value being defined in relation to some unit of division of the space in question;

2. *Relative value*, that is to say, value considered as the absolute value reproduced by addition to multiples of the module, from 1 to n times: each absolute value will have from 1 to n corresponding relative values;

3. *Fixed density of generation:* each original X will correspond to a Y of the same type and the same weight, the index of density being established as a fixed value between 1 and n;

4. *Mobile density of generation:* each X will correspond, by transformation, to a Y, of different type and weight.

This general definition can be explained by applying it, for example, to the system of pitches. Taking the pair: *absolute value* with the octave as module and the semitone as unit of division/*fixed density of generation*, with the index 1, the classical series of twelve sounds will be obtained. In fact, within the octave, there cannot be more than twelve semitones, on which the series is based, to the exclusion of all repetition; in each transposition (or a limited number of permutations) there will be a succession of *single* and *unique* sounds, which do not occupy the same position in any two series.

Ex. 1

I have defined a perfectly constituted and logically based formal world. I deliberately chose this simple example, so that the mechanism of deducing a series in relation to a given principle should be fully understood. To this series of absolute values, I can then apply a grid of relative values—tessitura—with the octave as module, so that a sort of 'ideal' original can be extended into the various fields delimited by the octave in the scale of audible sounds. Conversely, if my idea of the series be applied directly to relative values, it may or may not be reduced to absolute values; in other words, given a series whose elements are disposed in defined frequency-fields—defined by the octave, amongst other intervals—when the transpositions take place according to the proportions established between these relative values (the original intervals) my serial world will be perfectly defined. No 'reduction' to absolute values will be needed to justify its existence.

Ex. 2

Take another example: the case of a homogeneous complex of pitches. Suppose that groupings of absolute values are made (still in the domain of the semitone, with the octave as model) and that the result is a succession of complexes of variable density—still fulfilling the essential condition of non-repetition —:3/2/4/2/1, that is, all the twelve semitones of the octave.

If the ensemble of all the complexes is multiplied by a given complex, this will result in a series of complexes of mobile density, of which, in addition, certain constituents will be irregularly reducible; although *multiple* and *variable*, these complexes are deduced from one another in the most functional way possible, in that they obey a logical, coherent structure.

Ex. 3

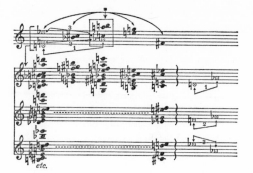

Here I shall merely outline a few further examples. Take the case of a non-homogeneous complex comprising pitch and duration; if the pitches are accorded durations directly (or inversely) proportional to the intervals which separate them, another form of generation will result from the order of the size of the interval being brought to bear on the order of succession.[1]

Ex. 4

In order to obtain very evolved ensembles, it will be advantageous to treat certain complexes by methods involving other complexes. The possibilities are infinitely vast and end in series having only a very distant relationship with the primitive series of twelve sounds.

[1] Each complex is multiplied by that shown in the rectangle, its transpositions being governed by the bracketed intervals; it should be noted that the resultant pitches are here treated as *relative* values. (Trans.)

Ex. 5

(A series deduced from Ex. 4, worked according to the procedures of Ex. 1 and 3.)

Moreover, there is no need to keep to *defined* objects; the concept of serial generation can equally well be applied to *fields*, provided that they obey the fundamental laws stated above. I can only really conceive of the musical world from the point of view of more or less limited fields; this is why I have never exaggerated the importance of the complete elimination of error in diagrams. The field in which a written pitch can be played is extremely narrow, and the risk of error is practically nil; with durations, the field is enlarged in proportion to the growth of margin of error; as for dynamics, they almost always occur in a field too wide for complete accuracy; in fact, like the point in geometry, a defined object can be considered as an extreme instance in the context of a field. Thus, musical thought can move in a world which evolves from existing objects to ensembles of probable objects.

Although the theory and mechanism of these operations may seem excessively abstract, they refer exclusively to the *concrete sound object*, for the properties of this object engender the structures and procure the formal qualities of the resultant

41

sound world. Nevertheless, it is no mere accident that these qualities and structural procedures depend on the concrete sound object: if that were the case the result would be a collection of permutating samples of accidents, observing no logical relationship other than this principle of permutation, a principle extrinsic to their overall characteristics. The danger of such a permutation of samples is especially present in the case of 'indeterminate' sounds—percussion, or, more generally, noise —whose individual complexity is inimical to a formal hierarchy which would reduce them to simple or at least relatively simple relationships.

This leads me to a digression on the relationships between noise and sound. Until now the hierarchy that has existed in the West has customarily excluded noise from its formal concepts; its use is apt to arise from an urge towards descriptive, paramusical illustration. This is not just a coincidence or a simple question of taste: Western music has long excluded noise because its hierarchy has depended on the principle of the identity of sound relationships which are transposable on all the degrees of a given scale; noise, being a phenomenon not directly reducible to another noise, is thus rejected as contradictory to the system. Now that we have an organism like the series, whose hierarchy is no longer based on the principle of identity by transposition, but, on the contrary, on localised and variable deductions, noise can be integrated more logically into a formal construction, provided that the structures responsible for it are based on its own criteria. They are not fundamentally different—acoustically speaking—from the criteria of a sound.

Let us experiment by giving a chord complex to an instrumental group of varied timbres. This complex is to be played during a very short space of time. When the phenomena related to the modes of attack are of a great intensity (strings at the heel of the bow, brass in the low register) this chord will be heard as a noise, rather than as an association of determinate sounds. Take, on the contrary, five drums and tap the skin of each one, in any order; the intervals which separate them are immediately perceptible, almost as if it were simply a matter of pitches. Thus, it is superficial to divide the sound phenomenon

42

into two such separate categories; it seems that sensations of noise and sound arise primarily from the greater or lesser selective analytical ability of the ear. When it hears a rapid succession of complex chords—particularly in the low register —or a single complex chord of extreme brevity, the ear is incapable of even an intuitive analysis of the relations between the pitches; it is saturated with complexity, and, *globally*, perceives noise. When it hears a reiterated succession of different noises in a simple and homogeneous context—the same family of instruments—it analyses them instantly and is able to specify, if only intuitively, the relations existing between them. (If the families are non-homogeneous, the sharpness of perception will again decrease, because it is dependent on analysis which is thus rendered difficult.) In my opinion, then, sounds and noises must be treated as a *function* of the formal structures which employ them, which *reveal* them for what they are, so to speak. Above and beyond the still naive idea of mixing the elements, there is a dialectic between structure and material, by virtue of which the one *reveals* the other.

Let us extend this idea from noise/sound relationships to crude sound/composed sound relationships. The dialectic of composition is more readily adapted to a neutral, not directly identifiable object, such as a pure sound or a simple aggregate of pure sounds that are not differentiated by internal functions of dynamics, duration or timbre. As soon as composed figures are fashioned into a 'formulated' complex, and used as basic objects of composition, they have of course lost all neutrality, and acquired a personality, an individuality, making them less suitable for a generalised dialectic of sound relationships. Crude sounds and composed sounds will *reveal* themselves by means of and as a function of the structures which bring them into play; it is not easy to discover the delicate point of balance between the responsibility of the structures and the personality of the objects. Moreover, 'noise' in its organic state can be reproduced at a more elaborate level by a 'formulated' sound-complex. On each side of 'pure sound', there are dangerous limits which have to be controlled if one is not to risk falling

43

from a true pitch series (simple or complex) to a permutation of samples.

Until now, I have only considered complexes of simple intervals; to complete the picture I must describe the *integration* of these same intervals. This method gives us, so to speak, sound 'surfaces' using either the true continuum or a rough approximation of this continuum by the aggregation of all the unitary intervals included within the given limits; these are called clusters in the vertical sense, or glissandi in the diagonal sense. Later on, we will see how this primitive and extremely summary idea is far from an elaborated conception of the continuum; here we have only the most superficial semblance of it. Clusters and glissandi could be called frequency bands: the glissando being used as a function of length of time, x to y, all the elements of the cluster functioning at a single time, x (the former a diagonal linear function of time, the latter a nullity of time). My previous remarks about defined objects and fields must be recalled in this connection; the frequency band represents a field completely filled with an amorphous material. Even though I may have justified the integration of the intervals into the hierarchy of pitch, and made it a function of time, it must be remembered that this will still be an extreme instance that is both amorphous and incapable of appearing in a context or a structure other than as a border-line case. In the last reckoning, these *clusters* and *glissandi* depend on a stylistic conception that is too elementary for my liking; their recent abuse has rapidly turned to caricature. This quickly 'parcelled' material is no guarantee of great acuteness of conception; it suggests, on the contrary, a strange weakness for being satisfied with undifferentiated acoustic organisms. Besides, speaking now not of style but of logic, these border-line cases cannot assume the properties of general cases without the necessary adaptation.

Still in connection with pitch, a further observation must be made. Whether a relative tessitura of absolute intervals is *applied* to a series developed within an interval of definition, or whether it is *integrated* into the actual development of the series, such a conception presupposes that the *guise* in which an interval appears differs from all its other *guises*, according to the tessitura which it adopts; from then on, the absolute interval of definition becomes the smallest common multiple of the actual, variable interval.

Without dwelling too long on the subject, we should mention the error of considering all the units of a basic organisation—the twelve semitones, in the case of the customary tempered system—as having to remain strictly and immovably equal amongst themselves: this would be an acoustic and structural absurdity, unless one sticks to a totally fixed succession in which tessitura is entirely renewed each time—and this cannot lead far. This misconception springs from a failure to understand the principle of *non-repetition* of the internal elements of the basic series; it has been confused with some mechanical or obsessional taboo on the recurrence of elements within structures, or outside the original organisation. As soon as one of the transformations of the original series is used, it goes without saying that this mechanical linking is immediately upset. On the other hand the advantage of transformations—or transpositions—lies in creating regions which are privileged in relation to others; the interplay of these functions of privilege can frequently sustain a dialectic of interconnection, entailing structural consequences which can be the basis of a form. In addition, when the elements are *placed* simultaneously in their relative tessituras, they follow or oppose the accoustic proportions 'of least resistance' (I am referring to simple relationships which we call the 'natural' harmonic series); from this very fact, they acquire reciprocal functions, the one corroborating or destroying, reinforcing or negating the other, and these give the material its internal profile, its energy potential, its malleability and its cohesive properties. These are all extremely important characteristics, whose structural consequences will be no less essential in the establishment of a form than those of serial linking. Thus, it is a mere illusion to conceive of sound points that are completely independent of a directional field—with certain clearly defined exceptions; a case in point is that of intervals, relative in tessitura, whose structures deny any functional principle of identity in the transpositions and

45

deformations which they undergo. An example will illustrate this principle of identity. In tonal language, a common chord in its root position has an identical function in all keys, major and minor, whatever its register, layout, and octave-doublings, provided it remains in root position. To compensate for the inadequacy of this principle in relation to natural resonance, there are a number of pragmatic interdicts or preferences concerning the good or bad disposition of chords and of writing in general. In the serial system, on the other hand, no function appears identical from one series to another, but each function depends solely on special characters and on their use; an object composed of the same absolute elements can, through the evolution of their placing, assume different functions. (The first and fourth movements of Webern's Second Cantata are, in this respect, especially clear; a comparison and an intrinsic study of these two movements will reveal this phenomenon, used with a simplicity of means which makes it clearly comprehensible.)

The 'avoided octave' is also included in this denial of the principle of identity. Again, a distinction must be made between the *actual* octave and the *virtual* octave. *Actual* octave relationships are established from point to point in a context of homogeneous coordinates: these are principally coordinates of durations, but also of dynamics or timbre. These *actual* octaves create a *weakening*, or *hole*, in the succession of sound relationships by way of provisionally reinstating a principle of identity denied by the other sounds, so that they are at variance with the principal of structural organisation of the world in which they appear; *actual* octaves must be completely avoided, at the risk of structural non-sense.

However, if we use a sound complex (still within a system of homogeneous coordinates) containing frequencies in octave or multiple octave relationships with the frequencies of another sound complex, these relationships are to be considered *virtual* octaves; the assimilation of the octave-forming sounds into their respective complexes is so strong that they cannot escape from the attraction of these complexes to impose their own principle of identity, and are incapable of giving

46

Ex. 6

even a fleeting impression of obeying such a principle: the complex has a pregnance[1] that overshadows that of the octave relationship.

Once certain acoustic precautions are taken, these *virtual* octaves do not create any structural or stylistic incongruity; these precautions are:

— On the one hand, avoid placing octave-forming notes at the extremities of sound complexes; since the simplest relationships are the most easily perceptible, the ear will immediately be drawn towards these octave-forming extremities.

Ex. 7

— On the other hand, when the sound complex is in an extended position, be sure to introduce one or more contradictory intervals, of greater tension, within the register bounded by the octave relationships. These intervals will weaken or annul the effect of octave relationships and will thus divert the ear from its tendency to simplify.

Nevertheless the existence of *virtual* octaves in point-to-point relationships can be considered when they occur in a system of non-homogeneous coordinates, principally with regard to the organisation of time (durations themselves or 'rates of flow'). The organisation of dynamics (and of timbre) has a weaker selective potential and a lesser pregnance. Suppose that a structure of points uses a given system of co-

---

[1] Or 'Prägnanz': c.f. Gestalt psychology. (Trans.)

Ex. 8

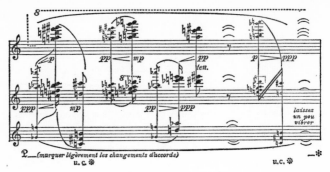

ordinates and that there is a simultaneous exposition of another structure of points having a different system of coordinates: another tempo, a non-assimilable organisation of pitch. The octave-relationships between these systems will be *virtual*: in the first place, the non-homogeneity of time will prevent these relationships from being perceived on the same level; by placing them in a different context, it will, on the contrary, reinforce the divergences between the structures in which they appear. Opposing dynamics and radically separated timbres will further emphasise the dieresis between them. The same acoustic precautions as before will naturally apply.

Complexes that are organised according to a system of non-homogeneous coordinates are correspondingly more likely to engender purely *virtual* octave relationships. I have already said that actual octaves create a weakening, or hole, in the succession of sound relationships; the same applies to common triads, not only when they appear in their own vertical dimension but also if they are the product of the superposition of several horizontal structures. As with octaves, they reinstate the principle of identity denied by all the other sounds; they are, in addition, 'charged with association(s)'. Their intrinsic meaning comes into conflict with the functions on which they depend: the disparity, in this case, is as much one of style as one of structure.

Ex. 9

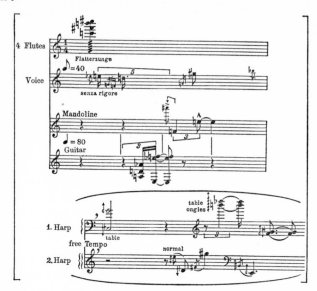

We will apply this general observation to all intervals, or combinations of intervals, which have a tendency to reinstate a functional principle of identity—of structural identification—in the dialectic of sound relationships: strongly gravitational intervals, combinations of intervals already assimilated into

Ex. 10

49

4

an established function. The octave and the triad are simply the most striking examples.

Finally, it must be stressed that absolute duration plays a primordial role in evaluating these relationships: a relationship that may be acceptable if it appears very briefly becomes intolerable if continued over a more extended period of time. It is once again a question of the laws of speed of perception; these will be studied later on, in connection with *striated* or *pulsed* time. The complexity or simplicity of the context is just as important as the part played by duration, and for the same reason: sharpness of perception. In a *rarefied* context, individual acoustic relationships are easy to grasp, consciously or intuitively, whereas in a more dense context, a rapid succession of events will prevent even an intuitive perception of most of the individual acoustic relationships. In the last resort, it is impossible to speak of laws governing pitch without mentioning their dependence on other formal criteria; I think this will be appreciated by all musicians who attach importance to the phenomenology of form.

We have studied in some detail the general serial system as applied to the particular case of pitch; now we come to duration. The problem here does not arise in exactly the same way, because the four categories that we have proposed are now enveloped by an over-riding property: tempo. Is this a completely new property, and does it apply exclusively to duration? Can tempo be compared to a field, to a tessitura of time in which a given set of phenomena occurs? Tempo is quite specific to duration; it is, as it were, the standard which will give a *chronometric* value to numerical relationships. It is comparable to total transposition in the domain of pitch; the transposition of an entire given structure on any interval amounts to choosing frequencies different from the initial ones, but obeying the same numerical relationships (once all corrections due to temperament have been allowed for). This operation modifies the perception of forms no less than a change of tempo. It is no less a caricature to play the Adagio of Beethoven's *Pathétique* Sonata three octaves higher or the end of Stravinsky's *Les Noces* three octaves lower than written, than to take a tempo three times as slow or three times as fast. Total transpositions of duration and pitch obtainable from magnetic tape have, in linking them automatically, made us aware in a general way of this aspect of tessitura. If, when speaking of pitch, I did not at first refer to transposition, it was because the numerical relationships of the frequencies (absolute or relative) which we notate are too complex to be easily shown other than as symbols; concerning duration, I started with the idea of tempo, because here we notate relatively simple *relationships* to which tempo can give quantitative definition. Tempo ought not to be conceived solely as a fixed standard; it is susceptible to a variability that may or may not be precisely determined. In the first case, passing from one fixed standard to another, *accelerando* or *ritardando* will result; in the second, the standard of duration will have a value undefined by any precise chronometric length of time: a global structure can then be inscribed in a chronometric field, whether defined or not. The boundaries of this chronometric field may be of two kinds: they may depend either on an abstract hierarchy or on an accidental hierarchy— a concrete acoustic phenomenon, the act of performance, or the psycho-physiological connection of these two facts (duration of vibration, time necessary for the performance of disjunct intervals, length of breath). This can be summarised in the following table.

Fixed tempo   Fixed standard

Mobile tempo   1. Directed; from fixed standard to fixed standard

             accelerando⎱ and the combinations of these
             ritardando ⎰ two directions

             Border-line case: from fixed standard to
                                  non-fixed standard or
                                  vice versa

        2. Non-directed; floating standard

          (a) Defined chronometric field
             abstract hierarchy
             accidental hierarchy

          (b) Non-defined chronometric field

We shall return later to the *properties* of these different tempi and the extent to which they are distinguished by the presence or absence of an internal pulse. Nevertheless, now that these different categories of tempo have been established, we can turn our attention to those relationships we call durations. The same division is established as for pitches: 1. absolute value, 2. relative value, 3. fixed density of generation, 4. mobile density of generation. A prefatory remark is necessary: accustomed as we are to the semitone, it seems we are concerned with a specific category of duration when multiplying and dividing the rhythmic unit, for the above operations are not carried out in the domain of pitch. Let us say that, from one organisation to the other, the importance of any phenomenon is displaced, as it is used in a different sense. Thus, in the domain of duration, one can start with the smallest value and multiply it to obtain the largest; by this method, a regular or irregular pulse is attained, reducible, in the latter case, to the figures 2 and 3, their sum, or their product.

Ex. 11

Equally, one can take the largest value as the unit and divide it into an even or odd number of regular parts; this is exactly the same operation as the preceding one, but in reverse.

Ex. 12

However, this method produces a regular pulsation of the unit, because the superposition of parts of these subdivisions cannot be imagined or realised in practice (Ex. 13).

If moreover the same subdivision is observed in all the structures, the unit can be altered by altering the tempo; the effect is as before (Ex. 14).

Ex. 13

Ex. 14

When the two methods are combined, a unit which is equally susceptible to multiplication and subdivision will be selected; the choice of tempo will be of prime importance to the perception of pulse as it is to the possibility of realising the subdivisions. With regard to pitch, a similar problem arises concerning the world of micro-distances, smaller than the semitone; if we think of the world of tempered chromaticism as being the multiplication of the semitone, micro-distances will be the division of this same unit by even or odd numbers.

The absolute values being chosen by the means just described, the relative values will be written in a defined tessitura, obtained by the multiplication or division of the basic scale, because the same methods apply on this superior level as with the unit itself. With regard to the density of generation, exactly the same terms are valid as for pitch. In addition, the possible modifications of a series of durations are of three kinds: fixed; mobile and non-evolutionary; mobile and evolutionary. 1. Fixed: the proportions of the original remain when they are multiplied or divided by a single numerical value; this is called augmentation or diminution. (It will not necessarily be a change in the ratio of 1:2, since it can also take place with irrational values.) 2. Mobile and non-evolutionary: the proportions of the original are modified by the addition or subtraction of a fixed value; instead of having a geometrical progression as before, one will have an arithmetical progression; the proportions will be enlarged or reduced irregularly, but always in the same direction. 3. Mobile and evolutionary: the proportions of the original are modified by a variable value, which is a fixed or mobile function of its (the original's) constituents, by, for example, 'dotting' all the values, whether or not they are already dotted: the automatic use of the dot results in irregularities because it sometimes adds a quarter, sometimes a half of the value.

Ex. 15

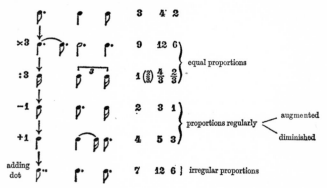

Moreover, the direction of the irregularities will not necessarily be constant.

From this, it is easy to deduce the mechanism of a simple series of durations. Example 16 shows the results produced by a complex of proportions. They are given in numerical form (and they will be transcribed in accordance with the two methods described above).

Ex. 16

$$\begin{bmatrix} 2 \\ 5 \\ 6 \\ 9 \end{bmatrix} \begin{bmatrix} 1 \\ 4 \\ 7 \\ 10 \end{bmatrix} \begin{bmatrix} 4 \\ 7 \\ 8 \\ 11 \end{bmatrix} \begin{bmatrix} 1 \\ 2 \\ 10 \\ 11 \end{bmatrix} \begin{bmatrix} 5 \\ 8 \\ 9 \\ 12 \end{bmatrix} \begin{bmatrix} 3 \\ 6 \\ 12 \end{bmatrix}$$

In the first transcription, I chose the semiquaver as the smallest basic unit and, by multiplication, I obtained the various values respecting the original global proportion;

54

Ex. 16a

in the second transcription, I chose the minim as the largest
basic unit and, by division, I obtained equal parts, whose sum
respects the original global proportion.

Ex. 16b

It now remains to place these values in relation to each
other, in other words, to distribute them within the field of
duration defined by the longest value; when this operation is
complete, a *block* of duration will thus have been formed, and a
diagonal dimension will have been introduced, which cannot be
confused with either the vertical or the horizontal dimensions.
Three types of distribution are possible: symmetrical, asymmetrical, and combined symmetrical-asymmetrical. Symmetrical distribution is regular if it takes place in relation to a
central axis (Ex. 17a), and again if the beginning or end of the
longest note is taken as the axis—all the notes starting or
finishing together (Ex. 17b, c).

In relation to a median axis, a directly contrary distribution
is seen to result if the durations are interrupted by complementary rests. In this case, silence no longer surrounds, pre-
cedes or follows the duration, but is introduced within it, thus
changing its character (Ex. 17d).

Naturally, it is possible to combine these elementary profiles
two by two, three by three or four by four, in order to

Ex. 17a–g

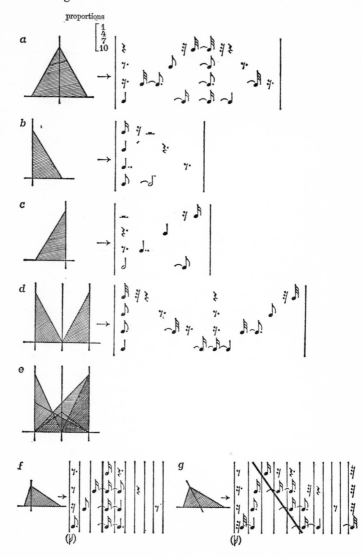

obtain more varied and less immediately definable blocks
(Ex. 17e). Symmetrical distribution will be irregular when it is
related to any other axis—whether straight or oblique (Ex.
17f, g); in relation to these axes, an equal (Ex. 17g) or unequal
(Ex. 17f) symmetry is of course possible. The distribution will
be asymmetrical when no axis is present.

Ex. 17h

If a block of this kind is proportionally divided it is clear that
ever more complex results will follow.

Ex. 17i

The same result will ensue from the application of a superior
category of distribution to the divided blocks. In addition,
'pockets' of silence can be imposed on a figure thus constituted,
filtering it, as it were.

Ex. 17k

Thus, whatever the point of departure, the two procedures
complement one another in creating a superabundance of

organisations of time, in both micro- and macro-structures. The rational use of the opposition between multiplication and division of the unit will, moreover, give rise to striking contrasts, due to the broader span of values brought into play.

All the methods of distribution within a duration block may be extended and applied to complexes of complexes, where each distributed element will no longer be a single value, but an ensemble; vast structures can then be formed, obeying the same principles of organisation in their constitution as in their disposition. The basic elements of these complexes of complexes will be either duration blocks, described above, or else whole series or divisions of series; interaction of these various methods of organisation can be extremely fertile, and will create an inexhaustible variety of objects—in the same way as in the field of pitch.

Finally, proportional complexes, defined above, can be applied to the tempo itself. This is not a forced or superficial extension since it is modelled on the subdivision of the unit. What is tempo, in fact? It is the inclusion of a greater or lesser number of units within a defined chronometric time. Consequently, if the chronometric unit is taken as the unit of value, its subdivision will give different tempi, observing the proportions of the numerical complex. As an example, take the complex 3/6/12, and the fifteenth of a second as the chronometric unit; each third of a unit will equal one forty-fifth of a second, each sixth one ninetieth, each twelfth one hundred-and-eightieth. Expressed in another way, our three units of tempo will be: $u = 45$, $u = 90$, $u = 180$ according to metronomic conversion (this unit being graphically chosen for its capacity to facilitate the transcription and execution of musical events). Simple series of fields in which events take place without being tied to more precise values may of course be used to counter this increasing complexity.

This idea can be enlarged to arrive at what I call true *time bubbles*, where only the proportions of the macro-structures are defined. This will give the whole range of durational properties, from the most precise and complex definition to the most summary of statistical phenomena. We will return later

Ex. 18

to the properties of statistical time and of evaluated, standard-ised time.

The idea of intervals of greater pregnance, as applied to pitch, can apply equally to duration relationships which, by their intrinsic qualities or their stylistic associations, are at variance with the time-world defined by the series; the evocation of a regular metre attracts particular attention, especially when it is repeated. I shall not repeat the reasons for this phenomenon, since they have already been explained at length.

We have now studied the morphological organisation of the two basic constituents of the sound phenomenon, pitch and duration, both functions of *integration*. Dynamics and timbre, functions of *coordination*, cannot claim the same rigour in their morphology, above all in music based on natural sounds. Dynamics are produced in a relatively large field, with a rather broad margin of indeterminacy; timbre uses constituted wholes—instruments or the voice—whose relationships are highly complex and irreducible to simple numerical proportions. Therefore, in general, reasoning must proceed by analogy. Only electro-acoustical means can assume a rigorous control over dynamics; with regard to timbre, they have not yet achieved convincing results. From this point of view, the scant interest of electronic realisations is due to the fact that the over-simplistic objects which are created do not contain a very rich multiplicity of transitory phenomena; starting from several elementary norms, a uniformity of acoustic events is produced. Electronic music ploughs the same furrows for lack of the perfected machines which would enable it to create differentiated timbres and to progress beyond white and coloured noise, aleatory modulations, etc. These elements become unbearable just as quickly as their equivalents, clusters and glissandi—similarly amorphous and undifferentiated.

Electro-acoustical means must leave the confines of the cobbler's workshop where they have got rather bogged down. Considering the rapid development of electronic techniques, such machines must shortly be produced; certain industrial projects have already made a start in this direction.

The organisation of dynamics, whether in the 'natural' or electro-acoustical field, is identical: in the second case, they are measured mechanically and, as a result, very exactly; in the first case, the margin of error implicit in the realisation of any scheme should be borne in mind: even if the scheme be strongly differentiated, a realisation of it will blunt its precision, soften its contours and give only an approximate 'interpretation' of the original; if rather more summary, the interpretation and the original will then be very close, because less reciprocally exacting. By virtue of this realistic view of things, one can choose a dynamic scale of greater or lesser precision, expressed by conventional symbols or—if the variability and scope of the dynamic field is to be stressed—by figures; in the first case, an *absolute* dynamic notation will result (in so far as such a thing is conceivable), and in the second, a deliberately relative, even invertible dynamic system.

A description of the details of this new organisation would be out of place here. It will be enough to mention the two categories on which it depends and which we will call: *point-dynamics* and *line-dynamics*. *Point-dynamics* mean that all dynamic degrees are fixed; one point will be linked directly to another on the chosen scale, without any intervening transition or gesture. *Line-dynamics*, on the other hand, involve the transitions from one given amplitude to another: crescendo, decrescendo and their combinations. This second category can be defined as a *dynamic glissando*, comparable to glissandi of pitch and of tempi (accelerando, ritardando). Notice, incidentally, that one's elementary psychology—whether one is musically educated or not—is instinctively aware of the close relation between glissandi of dynamics and tempo. It is extremely rare for a strong crescendo not to be matched by an appropriate accelerando or rallentando, depending on its formal functions—an agogic or suspensive climax, stretto or

cadence; it is equally rare for a steep diminuendo not to be
accompanied by a rallentando intended to 'distil' it; only the
liaison of decrescendo with accelerando does not seem in
accord with elementary psychology. In certain civilisations
—Bali, for example—we see, on the contrary, the independence
of conception of these two levels of sound-expression; but we
will return to this subject when we touch on interpretation.
Returning to the serial organisation of dynamics, we must add
that the *points* or the *lines* (with absolute or relative values)
will be ordered according to linear (simple series) or complex
functions (blocks of dynamics), obeying the same laws and
describable in the same ways as before. The distribution of
points, and above all of lines, will give way to symmetrical
(regular and irregular) and asymmetrical dispositions, and to
combinations of these various simple forms. The curves
previously drawn for pitch are applicable in full to the distribution of dynamics (Ex. 17).

It remains to specify the relationship of these organisms
with those responsible for pitch and duration. Just as a duration
can be manifested by a group of pitches (Ex. 19a), and a pitch

Ex. 19

can be realised within a group of durations, so use will be made
of a multiplicity of timbres, with a general dynamic envelope
(Berg, *Wozzeck*, Interlude on the note B (Ex. 20) between the

61

Ex. 20

second and third scenes of Act 3, bars 109—113) or with
individual curves (Ex. 19b).

Nevertheless, the relationships between these two organisms
will always be established from the simple to the simple, from
the simple to the complex, from the complex to the complex.
These relations are still valid for dynamics, but they will grow
to the level of the ensemble. While a single pitch cannot control
an ensemble of durations unless it employs several timbres, a
single intensity will do this very well and without any special
conditions;

Ex. 21

the new relations between dynamics on the one hand and pitch
and duration on the other, are established as follows: from
simple to ensemble,

Ex. 22

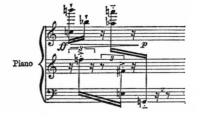

from simple to ensemble of ensembles,

Ex. 23

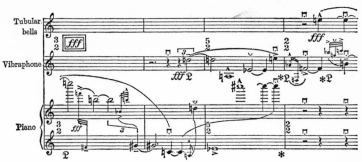

from complex to ensemble,

Ex. 24

from complex to ensemble of ensembles.

Ex. 25

Piano →

Xylophone
Bells →
Timp.

Woodwind →

(The dynamic schema of an extract from *Tombeau*.)

The symbols are variable and offer the following possible interpretations:

	a	b	c	d
6	*f*	*mf*	*pppp*	*ppp*
5	*mf*	*mp*	*ppp*	*pp*
4	*mp*	*p*	*pp*	*p*
3	*p*	*pp*	*p*	*mp*
2	*pp*	*ppp*	*mp*	*mf*
1	*ppp*	*pppp*	*mf*	*f*

It goes without saying that these dynamic signs represent fields and that these six degrees ought not to be taken as exact, but with a fairly accurate approximation of their proportions.

In addition, as for tessitura and tempo, registers of dynamics will be used. These registers will govern the ensemble of relative relationships set up in detail from object to object. Finally, the compositional precautions taken are now of a different kind; they are concerned with certain acoustic results: masking effects between neighbouring tessituras marked with extreme dynamics, the acoustic density of pitch complexes marked with divergent dynamics, etc. A number of these pragmatic measures will be in the sphere of instrumentation.

In the world of *natural* sound, timbre, as we have said, is presented in the form of constituted ensembles. What is an instrument, in fact—what is the voice for that matter—if not an ensemble constituted of timbres of limited evolution within a given tessitura? Treatises on instrumentation, even if they do not give this definition, have always put it into practice; they give the tessituras of instruments, and the different means of playing them (without mute, with mute, pizzicato, arco, etc.); they then describe how the instrument reacts to these various kinds of treatment according to the tessitura and the dynamic ambitus. Unlike amplitude, timbre cannot alter gradually; at best, the illusion can be created by imperceptible variations within complexes of timbres.

To clarify the use of this sound dimension, it will be separated into two families:

1. *non-evolutionary* or, at least, *of limited and homogeneous evolution* (the same timbre or same group of timbres);

2. *evolutionary and non-homogeneous:*

(a) proceeding by *disjunct intervals*, so to speak (passing from one instrument to another, from one homogeneous group to another, from one non-homogeneous complex to another, where the weight of the new timbres is greater than that of the timbres common to the two; passing from an instrument to any group, from a homogeneous to a non-homogeneous group);

(b) proceeding by *conjunct intervals* (passing from one non-homogeneous complex to another, where the weight of the new timbres is less or equal to that of the timbres common to the two; passing from a timbre to a modification of the same timbre).

Of course, these intervals will be more or less disjunct according to the relative difference of timbre in the succession of instruments or groups, whether homogeneous or non-homogeneous; they will be more or less conjunct, according to whether the weight of the common timbres is appreciably less than or bordering upon that of the new timbres. The timbres too will be ordered according to linear or complex functions. Timbre has a very special role: it frequently articulates pitch and dynamics, at the intersection of these two dimensions; it may also articulate pitch and duration (Ex. 19b) and, more rarely, dynamics and duration (also Ex. 19b). As with dynamics, its relations with the other structures will be established not only from element to element, but from one element to an ensemble of elements; all the combinations described in the preceding paragraphs need not be repeated.

5

Such organisations of timbres will of course take into account both the micro- and the macro-structures; they are involved in the description of the object, or rather its fabrication, while placing it in a coherent overall ensemble of objects. In electro-acoustic invention, families of timbres are susceptible to the same classification as instrumental and vocal families; but it is possible, theoretically, to pass from one timbre to another without a break in continuity. It would be premature and presumptuous to try to infer more from the works and experiments at present known to us. Likewise, we are reduced to supposing that differentiated timbres can be formed; this goal will not be attained by imposing dynamic envelopes upon superposed frequencies any more than by reducing sums of frequencies. Calling on vague notions of statistical distribution will not replace a close study of transitory phenomena— both the initial attack and the sound itself—and the rational application of the laws deduced from such study. Scientists appear to be working to the greater benefit of musicians, who are condemned to remain amateurs in this field.

There remains a fifth dimension, which is not, strictly speaking, an intrinsic function of the sound phenomenon, but rather its *index of distribution*: I refer to space.[1] Unfortunately it was almost always reduced to altogether anecdotal or decorative proportions, which have largely falsified its use and distorted its true functions. (It is not for nothing that Berlioz and the Venetians, respectively the most outgoing and the most decorative of composers, are always cited as its ancestors.) Is space no more than a clockwise or anti-clockwise mannerism? The abuse of such *space-glissandi* seems to me to originate from an aesthetic just as summary as the immoderate use of clusters, glissandi and other types of white noise, not to

[1] The first public concerts using spatially mobile sound-sources took place in Paris in 1951–52. Following a procedure worked out by Schaeffer, either three fixed channels or a mobile circuit on the three channels could be used. I myself wrote a study using these possibilities, starting from two fixed and one mobile circuit. Stereophonic sound in cinemas also dates from the same period (*Cinerama in New York*, late 1952), as do the *Son et Lumière* displays. Thus, commercial and industrial applications appear to be approximately on a par with more disinterested researches.

mention their inconvenient tendency to recall realistic movements much too faithfully—properties which commercial
manipulators have not failed to exploit. I personally cannot
accept such a simplistic view; spatial distribution seems to
me to merit a type of writing just as refined as the other sorts of
distribution already encountered. It ought not only to distribute
spaced-out ensembles according to simple geometric figures,
which after all always turn out to be contained in a circle or an
ellipse: equally—and in fact even more so—it must order the
micro-structure of these ensembles. While speed of displacement has always been stressed above all, little attention,
amounting almost to total neglect, has been paid to the
properties of statistically distributed objects linked in a
circuit, or of mobile objects.

It is obvious that the index of distribution, space, acts not
only on the durations, but also on pitch, dynamics and timbre
within the time-span; static or mobile distribution can be
considered as maintaining certain relationships with all these
interacting characteristics. These relationships are of greater
subtlety than those of simple speeds—angular or lateral
according to the spatial lay-out in use, even leaving out of
account the *local* acoustical conditions, which seriously com-
plicate the problem. Thus, these large distributions and space
glissandi can again be imagined as extreme instances whose
lack of finesse, analytically speaking, denies the possibility of
self-renewal. They hardly deviate from the primary typology
of the Venetians and of Berlioz, that is to say, from a typology of
cardinal points—a symbolism openly acknowledged in the
latter's *Requiem*. It seems to me that the real interest in distribution lies in the creation of 'Brownian movements'[1] within a
mass, or volume of sound, so to speak; hence it is a question of
elaborating a strongly differentiated typology of relationships,
to be set up between the phenomenon itself, whether individual
or collective, and its actual, *absolute* place in real space.

Here we must briefly attempt to define the situation of the
listener, a definition which will be further developed in the

[1] *Brownian movements:* the random motions of particles suspended in
fluid, due to the thermal motions of the molecules of the fluid. (Trans.)

chapter on aesthetics and poetics, since the position of the listener in relation to the musical fare offered him belongs less to acoustics, strictly speaking, than to the psycho-physiology of listening. The listener will be placed outside or inside the area within which the sound events occur. In the first case, he will observe the sound, in the second, he will be *observed* by the sound, surrounded by it. (It is this duality of position that I attempted in the spatial lay-out of *Poésie pour pouvoir*, where a spiral lay-out allowed the alternation and combination of both contingencies.)

Consider the two families: *fixed distribution, mobile distribution*—which I also refer to as static relief and dynamic relief. To return to a classification used with regard to timbres, *mobile distribution* will take effect by conjunct and disjunct movements. It must be stressed that these terms, conjunct and disjunct, are not solely dependent on actual distance, nor even on proportionate distance; they are dependent both on the *overlapping* of the phenomena displaced—an extrinsic property of positioning—and on the properties of these phenomena. I will explain: take two identical chords, each having an equal duration, dynamic and timbre; thus, in principle, they are strictly equivalent. The first chord is played at a given point in space, the second at some distance from this point; if the first is still sounding at the moment of entry of the second, and dies away to reveal it, the result is what I call a conjunct interval; the time of superposition is the time necessary for the ear to become accumstomed to the passage from one to the other. The more I curtail this interval of time, until it equals zero, the stronger will be the impression of displacement. After this point a silence will intervene between the two chords; at first it will be a short silence, in which the impression of displacement will be at its maximum; this I call a disjunct interval. As the silence becomes longer, the ear will expect a new event, the continuity will be broken, and the impression of displacement will become weaker, or even non-existent: there will no longer be any relationship, hence no interval. The distance will be accentuated by contrasting dynamics, whereas a unifying dynamic which includes the two chords in the same

68

curve will help the displacement, will almost materialise it. If they have totally different timbres, and extremely unequal duration, the disparity will again be increased. The interval will be more and more disjunct. An infinite number of variations can arise from the opposition of identical and divergent characteristics; the actual *absolute* value of the distance will be considerably enhanced. These conjunct and disjunct intervals will, in general, give continuous displacements of lines or discontinuous leaps between points; these two categories can be applied from unit to unit, from unit to group, and from groups to groups.

Up till now, I have considered 'ideally' executed transitions between fixed sound sources; the network of possibilities already studied can be thought of as extending to mobile sound sources, but the 'gestural' activity presupposed by this extension—at least when it concerns instrumentalists and singers—poses another problem, this time of aesthetics. For the moment it seems that the theatre alone can justify all the gestures concomitant with a mobile source. This does not mean a theatricalised concert—which would end up as debased theatre, bereft of all literary and dramatic qualities—but a theatre integrating speech, sound and colour by means of gestures; the No theatre is an admirable traditional example of this idea. (This comparison indicates how much I am opposed to all *gesticulation* in my own idea of a mobility of sources. Recent experiments have utterly convinced me that all *gesticulation* immediately kills the attention owed to the structures themselves, producing the opposite of the result intended—and gesticulation in sound has the same effects. We will return to this.)

A fixed spatial lay-out represents in the *arrested* state what a spatial lay-out offers kinematically; in this case conjunct and disjunct intervals, obeying the same criteria, are fixed, once and for all. Fixed as well as mobile lay-outs—commanding fixed and mobile sources—observe the elementary laws of regular or irregular symmetry, of asymmetry, and of the combination of these two forms. Naturally, when we speak of symmetry and asymmetry, we include both the properties of

69

the sound sources and the nature of the leaps or transitions taking place between them: two groups will be symmetrical if they are situated at an equal distance from an axis of some kind; if they possess homogeneous or non-homogeneous timbres, identical in quality and density, they can be considered as regularly symmetrical; they are irregularly symmetrical if their homogeneity is not of the same nature (a group of brass against a group of strings, for example) or if their non-homogeneity differs in quality and in density; they will otherwise be asymmetrical. Whatever the nature of the units or the ensembles to which they apply, the transitions or leaps will be symmetrical or asymmetrical.

The functions of articulation assumed by space as an index of the distribution of structures are, in fact, very close to those assumed by dynamics and timbres in relation to pitch and duration. Thus the sound phenomenon is seen in a quite unaccustomed light; we have studied it as a true *phenomenon* whose functions are reciprocally enveloping and enveloped, being integrated in the production, organisation and distribution of infinitesimal structures, as in the generation, coordination and disposition of overall structures. The extension of this method leads to equally radical perspectives on the concept of form.

I cannot end this morphological study without drawing attention to two important points:

1. the internal structure of a series which determines potential transformations and its connecting links within a single dimension;

2. the way in which the interaction of the different sound components manifests itself, both qualitatively and quantitatively.

The internal structure of a series is crucial in the development of its organisational potential; consequently it should not be left to chance; on the contrary, it is necessary to foresee the precise direction in which these powers are to be deployed. These structures will be of two kinds: symmetrical or asymmetrical. Symmetry will depend on parallel, retrograde, inverted and inverted retrograde elements; these can undergo such regular transformations as permutation of the elements and augmentation of intervals.

A series is totally symmetrical when it can be broken down into a greater or lesser number of isomorphic figures. Webern's series, for example, are always of this kind, the figures being two, three or four in number, according to whether they comprise six, four or three notes in the scale of twelve tempered semitones; the series of Opus 24 may be quoted as perhaps the clearest example of this type, because it is easily reducible; but the series from Opus 28 would do just as well, and is almost more schematic.

Ex. 26

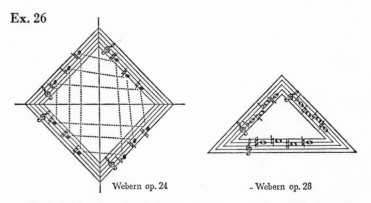

Webern op. 24   .. Webern op. 28

The initial series of Berg's *Lyric Suite* contains all the possible intervals, the last five being a symmetrical inversion of the first five—pivoting around the diminished fifth, the only non-invertible interval.

Ex. 27

Other series possess partial symmetries: they include both isomorphic figures—sometimes having elements in common

71

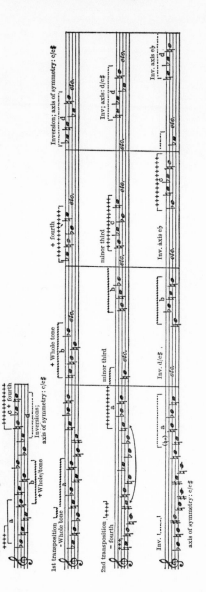

—and non-isomorphic figures. The series of the *Allegro misterioso*, also from Berg's *Lyric Suite*, provides the prototype.

The same figure recurs four times, presenting the notes in identical intervallic relationships, but in a different order of succession (B♭A♮F♮B♮; B♮C♮G♮D♭; D♮E♭E♮B♭), or in inverted intervallic relationships and in a different order of succession (A♭D♮E♭E♮). These figures are reduced to the same proportions

F♮ G♮ B♭ A♭ A♮ B♮ D♮ E♮ B♭ C♮ E♭ E♭ B♮ D♭ E♮ D♮ .[1]

They have several notes in common (B♭; B♮; D♮; E♭; E♮). In this case note that the isomorphic figure is continuous each time it appears (the four notes follow without interruption); this will be called manifest partial symmetry. The contrary case, concealed partial symmetry, will apply to isomorphic figures which are discontinuous. An example of this is formant 2, *Trope*, from my Third Piano Sonata.

The series is divided into four groups, of four, one, four and three notes respectively, which I will call a, b, c, d. Groups a and b/d are joined isomorphically, the original figure a being at the same time inverted and permutated; group c consists of two isomorphic figures. Figure a is reducible to two generative intervals, the semitone and the fourth, which will create the vertical and horizontal relationships (E♮–F♮/B♭–F♯; E♮–B♮/F♮–F♯); the connecting intervals are the augmented fourth and the whole tone (F♮–B♮; F♯–E♮). In the figure b/d obtained by inversion and permutation, the vertical relationships are the augmented fourth and the whole tone (G♯–D♮/C♯–E♭); the horizontal relationships and the connecting intervals being the semitone and the fourth (G♯–D♯/D♮–E♭; D♮–C♯/E♭–G♯). Figure c is composed of two isomorphic elements, minor thirds (G♮–B♭/C♮–A♮) observing globally the transposition of a whole tone (G♮–A♮/B♭–C♮); but if the

---

[1] The intervals between terms in successive groups are major third, minor second and minor second; but the last term in each is part of an *inversional* progression. (Trans.)

Ex. 29a

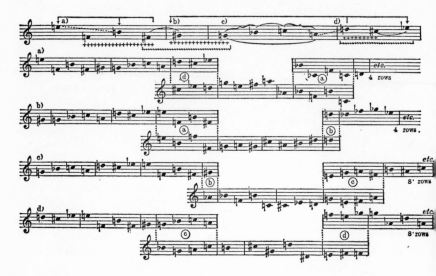

notes obtained by inversion are seen in apposition to those of the original figure the relationship of the semitones and the fourth will again be found (G♮–C♮; B♭–A♮). Finally, the series is composed of two isomorphic figures: a/bd, and of a group which itself includes two isomorphic figures: c; this last group—which is *divisible—divides* the second isomorphic figure bd into two unequal parts: b (one note, G♯) and d (three notes: D♮C♯E♭). Thus there is, on the one hand, manifest symmetry within c and, on the other hand, concealed symmetry between a and the two fragments b, d. In addition the intervals which relate the groups to each other are the same as the fundamental intervals of the groups: whole tone, semitone and fourth.

A single series can obey several isomorphic laws. A figure of three notes (e.g. B♮B♭D♮) may undergo an augmentation (E♭C♯A♮) in which all its intervals are doubled, and then appear in a symmetrical, retrograde form (G♯E♮F♮); finally, to complete the twelve notes, a figure is added which is irreducible to the principal figure.

Ex. 29b

Ex. 30a

What do we notice? Other isomorphic relationships result
from this triple succession of three-note isomorphic figures.
There are two four-note figures linked by very obvious relationships; these include a pair of intervals a, separated by another
interval b, a and b being interchanged from the first to the
second group. The first pair of intervals, two minor seconds
(B♮–B♭/D♮–E♭), is separated by a major third; the second
pair, two major thirds (C♯–A♮/G♯–E♮), is separated by a
minor second (A♮–G♯). The minor seconds are inverted in
relation to each other (descending and ascending seconds),
whereas the major thirds are parallel (descending); moreover,
one of the central intervals that act as axes of symmetry is
ascending, the other descending. The third four-note figure
is irreducible. Once more let us take the same three-note
figure; this time it will be augmented, then inverted, and to
complete the twelve notes, another irreducible figure will be
added to it.

75

Ex. 30b

What do we notice now? Two isomorphic figures, each of
five notes, the second of which is the retrograde of the first;
the last three notes correspond to the first three, by retrograda-
tion (B♮B♭D♮–G♯E♮F♮); from the pivotal third note, the
retrograde is combined with inversion of the intervals (D♮E♭C♯–
A♮G♮G♯). The final figure of two notes (C♮F♯) is apparently
irreducible to the other two. Notice, however, that the interval
between the last note of the second figure and the first of these
terminal notes is the same as that between the second of these
two notes and the first note of the first figure (F♮–C♮/F♯–B♮);
if the second note (F♯) is placed at the beginning of the series,
we shall have two six-note isomorphic figures. This series will
obey two different isomorphisms; the first, partial, forming
three figures; the second, total, forming two.

Ex. 30c

Finally, there are totally asymmetrical series; these occur
principally when a limited number of elements is used, because
isomorphic elements are almost inevitable, even if only of a
single interval or a given proportion, as soon as the number of
basic elements increases.

In conclusion, there are three distinct types of serial structure:

— totally symmetrical
— partially symmetrical and asymmetrical
    manifest isomorphic figures
    concealed isomorphic figures
— totally asymmetrical.

76

It is possible to pass from one to another of these families by means of altering the original. Sometimes minimal alterations will be enough to change the type of a series. In the *Lyric Suite*, Berg passes from the totally symmetrical series of the first movement (divisible into two isomorphic figures—Ex. 27) to the partially symmetrical series of the third movement (with four isomorphic figures—Ex. 28, second transposition). This is effected by the exchange of two notes that occupy parallel rather than symmetrical positions in the series (F♯ and A♮). All the properties of the original are thereby radically modified.

The characteristics just described are applicable to all numerical relationships and can have various applications.

If I have dwelt at length on the structure of the series itself, it is because it forms the basis of the entire organisation of series derived from it, the initial figures recurring only in certain transpositions, depending on the interval which separates the transposition of the original isomorphic figures, or the transformation taking place between them (inversion, retrograde or their combination). This group of series, in which figures from the original series recur, will be called 'privileged'. In every serial system, there is a network of series which are privileged in relation to an original series; when the original is changed, the network is changed correspondingly; each series is thus part of a privileged network, which has a certain number of identical (and no longer merely isomorphic) figures in common.

In the case of totally symmetrical series, there will be as many privileged transpositions as there are isomorphic figures in the original. In the case of the series from Webern's Opus 24 (Ex. 26) there are, apart from the original series, three other series possessing exactly the same figures. These form a network of four series, having four symmetrical figures in common, and these are the only possible series which include all four figures on these precise pitches.

All the transpositions of this serial structure will, as a result, be reducible to six networks of four series each; these six networks will be based on the six transpositions of the first figure which lead from position a to position b.

Ex. 31a

Ex. 31b

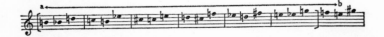

In the case of partially symmetrical series, an intervallically exact figure from the original will recur in as many derived series as there are isomorphic figures. Take the series of Berg's *Allegro misterioso* (Ex. 28). Figure a is found three more times in the original: in b, it is transposed a tone higher; in c, transposed a fourth higher; in d, it is inverted in relation to an axis C♮–C♯. As a result, figure a recurs in permutation b when the original series is transposed down a tone, in permutation c when it is transposed down a fourth, in d when it is inverted in relation to the axis C♮/C♯. Berg uses only this one family; but the network itself is more extensive. Figure b is also found in three transpositions, as are figures c and d. Thus, there is a global network of thirteen series (four times three derived series, plus the original) in which the four figures a, b, c and d recur.

By means of this ambiguity, isomorphic figures can create privileged linking functions as well as series of privileged networks. The series quoted in Ex. 29a, begins each time with a different group: a, b, c, d: and the last group is used as a linking figure; leaving aside the question of permutation the first group of the new series must thus be identical with the last of the preceding series. If I start from a, the identical

78

figures will always be d and a; starting from b, a and b; starting from c, b and c; from d, c and d. In this instance the concept of circular permutation has given rise to cyclic links of a different nature, depending on the constantly renewed conjunction of two isomorphic figures. This same principle was to generate the overall form of *Trope*, which is simply an enlarged circular permutation.

If a series contains two isomorphic families, it will form part of a double network of privileged series (Ex. 30c). These possibilities have already been demonstrated clearly enough in the two preceding cases for the reader himself to be able to deduce the derivatives from the original series.

Until now, we have considered the symmetrical or asymmetrical characteristics of a basic series, whose properties generated privileged networks or ensembles of privileged networks. But a non-symmetrical original can give rise to isomorphic objects; we will examine a particular case. Divide a series into five totally asymmetrical objects: a b c d e; object a is composed of m notes, object b, n notes, etc. In order to obtain new objects, the whole is multiplied by each of its parts in turn.

Ex. 32 (see also Ex. 3)

$$
\begin{array}{l}
\quad\quad a^{\{m}\ b^{\{n}\ c^{\{p}\ d^{\{q}\ e^{\{r} \\
\hline
m\times \left[aa\quad ab-ac-ad-ae \right] \\
n.\times \left[ba\quad bb\quad bc-bd-be \right] \\
p\times \left[ca\quad cb\quad cc\quad cd-ce \right] \\
q\times \left[da\quad db\quad dc\quad dd\quad de \right] \\
r\times \left[ea\quad eb\quad ec\quad ed\quad ee \right]
\end{array}
$$

Thus, series having multiple isomorphic relationships are created; in addition, there will be as many series as the object has notes: m first series, n second series, etc. As a result, the number of totally isomorphic objects will increase in direct proportion to the number of pitches constituting the original object. If an object a of three notes is multiplied by an object e of two notes, five totally isomorphic objects will result: (ae) 1, 2, 3 and (ea) 1, 2.

Ex. 33

Partially isomorphic objects will be those having an original object in common; all the objects in b, for example, will have the common structure b, while the other structure will be variable: ab, bb, cb, db, eb. Only the 'pure' objects, that is to say, those multiplied by themselves: aa, bb, etc., are totally asymmetrical in relation to each other. In point of fact three types of relationships can be found between the objects thus deduced from an original structure: totally isomorphic objects, partially isomorphic objects and non-isomorphic objects. If this procedure is extended to relationships in general, we realise the importance of finding methods of generation which can create networks of privileged relationships between the objects to which they give rise.

Finally, symmetrical structures are of two types, being produced in relation either to a centre or to an axis. Numerically, their application is straightforward, but they are no less easily transcribed into terms of pitch.

Ex. 34

Two intervallic families appear here: the major second, the major third, the augmented fourth; the minor second, the minor third, the fourth. The rational use of these two families is of prime importance if use is to be made of the symmetry of elementary figures in the internal structure of a series and the functions which derive from it; this is illustrated by Ex. 29.

Until now, we have examined what might be called 'complete' series. From these higher organisations, it is possible to deduce partial structures, which will be called *limited* series and *defective* series; both are obtained by a *reduction* of the original. In the case of limited series, this reduction will be structural, in the case of defective series, the procedures will be mechanical. *Limited* series can only result from totally symmetrical series; they do not use all the isomorphic figures which constitute the original series, but retain only some of them, or even only a single figure. In this way continuity in the linking of figures can be interrupted, otherwise the linkage would continue to make use of a single sequence of transformations of a given figure in relation to its isomorphisms. From the series of Webern's Opus 28 (Ex. 26), a single figure can be extracted

Ex. 35

and freed from the transposition and the inversion to which it is usually linked; since it forms a continuous fragment of the chromatic complement, its relationships with the other figures will be of little concern, since these relationships will necessarily be chromatic. If, as in the majority of cases, the chosen figure did not form a continuous fragment of the chromatic complement, the relationships linking one figure to another would have to respect the essential condition of chromatic complementarity.

Defective series are deduced by applying to the original series a mechanical procedure such as changing the module or 'filtering' the frequencies; this filtering systematically modifies a frequency, and may even replace it by an absence of sound. A change of module is, so to speak, a structural feature independent of the structure of the series, thus modifying it automatically. Take the series quoted in Ex. 1: its ambit is a major seventh; now reduce this by half, to a fourth. When we take each of the two fourths which make up the major seventh in turn, two—complementary—defective series will be obtained.

These transformations are extremely important if continuous use of the whole of the chosen sound-spectrum is to be avoided; they are particularly indispensable in the sphere of duration and

Ex. 36

dynamics. Here, the constant use of an extended scale of values is statistically bound to cause a lack of differentiation which is particularly intolerable in this context. The filtering of frequencies must similarly have a structural justification (axis of symmetry, privileged family of intervals) but it will thereafter be applied automatically, like a change of module: a note or a group of notes will be changed into other notes or groups of notes according to certain laws; it may perhaps be replaced by silence: thus suppressed, the structure forms, as it were, the background of that which remains. This filtering may apply equally to numerical relationships; negative structures can usefully result, making their reappearance in a positive form still more forceful.

It is hardly necessary to state that these reductions of the original series are eminently variable and mobile, and that they can occupy determinant roles; they have the effect of breaking down the rigidity which arises from the exclusive use of primary structures. Limited and defective series make the mechanisms of derivation considerably more supple, and at the same time they enlarge the field of variation.

Some important questions immediately spring to mind: how can series applied to the different characteristics of the sound phenomenon be organised with respect to each other? Must they be of like construction? Have they the right to be independent and to interact from different perspectives? These questions will be answered later, when we touch on syntax itself.[1] But first we must return to a study of the world in which serial laws are implemented.

In concluding this theoretical study of the series, however, I must stress one very important point: the series is not an arbitrary generative element, since it is based on definite and important properties of an ensemble of sounds. As soon as one

[1] Pp. 99–142.

series is chosen in preference to another, by virtue of its more or less selective capacities for musical organisation, the entity defined by the original series likewise precludes the arbitrary, since all inferences from it are necessarily linked to a selection based on the realities of sound. Neither will the composer himself make arbitrary use of the individual series in the resultant ensemble: he makes a choice, a fresh selection, from among those series presenting a greater or lesser number of outstanding properties or common relationships. There is a confusion between the statement (even permutated) or display of a certain number of sound phenomena, and the organisatory potential of their hierarchy. This confusion is still the basis of many discussions that are irrelevant to a truly musical reality.

MUSICAL SPACE

I have tried to give a fairly general survey of the idea of the series and to show some of its various applications. Perhaps I may now refer back to the quotation on axiomatic method by Louis Rougier, given in the first chapter: 'One single form may apply to diverse material, to groups of differing objects, provided only that these objects respect the same relationships amongst themselves as those present among the undefined symbols of the theory.' In order to promote a generalised theory of the series, it is expedient to define the true characteristics of the sound world which it will govern; we ought, accordingly, to find common criteria for the constituents of this world and their environment. We must, after all, extend our horizons to include new and unknown worlds as well as those to which we are accustomed.

In the domain of pitch, our definition of the series is applicable to any tempered space, according to any temperament, and to any non-tempered space, according to any module, whether it be the octave or some other interval. It seems to me that one of the most urgent objectives of present-day musical thought is the conception and realisation of a *relativity* of the various musical spaces in use. Western civilisation has brought polyphony to a high degree of perfection; to this end, a simplification, a 'standardisation' of intervals respecting general 'norms' has been imposed. However, the time has obviously come to explore variable spaces, spaces of mobile definition capable of evolving (by mutation or progressive transformation) during the course of a work. On the one hand this variability of musical space is associated with the complexity and density of the internal structure, the interlinking, distribution or superposition of the sound phenomena, which, by dispersion or saturation, prevent the perception of strongly differentiated intervals. It is associated, on the other hand, with the general tempo governing the pace at which the structures are expounded, since the ear needs time for the perception of intervals if it is to appreciate them. Finally it is associated with the proportional relationships between intervals, a subtle modification from one quantity to another being more perceptible, the more limited the field in which it operates. (These remarks are valid for all organisations: duration, dynamics and timbres, as well as pitch.) In addition, the exploration of intervals based on a unitary value less than the semitone is closely dependent on instrumental or vocal practice—both the technique of performers and that of instrument makers; no interval equal to or less than a quarter-tone, for example, will be perceptible if it is played or sung with vibrato: this will 'hide' the interval, being of a similar size. Mobile definitions of musical space thus imply theoretical antecedents which must be more precisely defined, no less than practical consequences in performance; these must be tackled, even to the extent of modifying the instruments which rule us at present, and adopting those which are capable of mobility in their adaptation to the various phases of unity on which evolutionary musical space would depend.

We have stressed the variability of space, starting from mobile definitions, whether tempered or not. This extremely important point must be examined in more detail, because it leads on the one hand to the concept of the continuum, on the other hand to the qualitative definition of musical space, considered, for the moment, only from the point of view of pitch. It seems to me of prime importance to define 'continuum' first of all. This is certainly not the transition *'effected'* from one point in space to another (successive or instantaneous). The continuum is *manifested* by the possibility of *partitioning* space according to certain laws; the dialectic between continuity and discontinuity thus involves the concept of partition; I will go so far as to say that continuum *is* this possibility, for it contains both the continuous and the discontinuous: partition, in fact, simply changes the aspect of the continuum. The finer partition becomes, tending towards an epsilon of perception, the more it will tend towards true continuity, this being not only a physical, but above all a physiological limit. Frequency-space may undergo two sorts of partition: the one, defined by a standard measure, will be regularly repeatable, the other, imprecise, or more exactly, undetermined, will occur freely and irregularly. Temperament—the choice of a standard measure—will be an invaluable aid in estimating an interval; in short, it will *'striate'* the surface, the musical space, and will provide our perception—even if it is far from totally conscious—with useful points of reference; in the opposite cases, where partition can be effected at will, the ear will lose all landmarks and all absolute cognisance of intervals; this is comparable to the eye's inability to estimate distances on a perfectly smooth surface. The properties of the partition determine the micro-structural properties of the smooth or striated space, and the way it is perceived; in extreme cases smooth and striated space fuse into a continuous line. This fusion is predictable as a result of the ambiguity which makes it easy to see-saw from one to the other. Indeed, the disposition of palpably equal-proportioned intervals within a smooth space will lead the ear to relate them to a striated space; likewise, in striated space, intervals which are very dissimilar in proportion will be detached from their temperament by one's perception, and thought of as being within a smooth space: in both cases, there is a pregnance[1] of the 'accidental' arrangement in relation to the organising principle. With these distinctions, whose

[1] See footnote, p. 47; the 'accidental arrangement' forms a 'Gestalt'. (Trans.)

subtlety, far from being gratuitous, is based on reality itself, we have come a long way from defining the continuum solely in its extreme instances as a continuous line or as a total, an integration.

Once the concept of partition is understood, we can encompass the macro-structural properties of space. To take this idea still further: can partition be produced regularly in the general ambit of audible sounds? Must the module, within which partition is brought to bear on the generative series, be fixed, or can it vary? Is it possible to conceive of space as partly smooth, partly striated? These questions must be answered using radically new definitions of space. Until now, definition of a module has been based exclusively on the proportion 2:1; in other words the octave is the archetypal definition of space, reinforced by the principle of identity which tonality perpetuated. Serial construction has adopted this archetype without special consideration; however, if the notion of space is to be enriched and, above all, to be rid of this identity-by-reproduction so uncritically inherited, then this simple doubling factor must be considered inadequate. If the octave is avoided in formulated structural relations, logic demands a means to dispose of the very principle; in other words, the appearance of the actual octave will be easily avoided within a space which it no longer organises.

Thus, a difference has been created between straight and curved space. *Straight spaces* will be those whose unvarying module reproduces the basic frequencies over the whole range of audible sounds; this module can of course be any interval. The octave, one particular case, will be the limit, larger intervals being only the preceding intervals added to it. The total ambit of the frequencies will contain this basic module a certain number of times, dividing it into a determined number of equal fields. *Curved spaces* will be those which depend on a regularly or irregularly variable module: if this module is regularly variable, the curved space will be focalised; irregularity of the module will result in a non-focalised curved space. The *defining* module in terms of which all the others are to be *defined*, will be called the focus. When the focus of a focalised

86

curved space is placed at any point of the ambit, partially symmetrical spaces will result; total symmetry will prevail when the focus is placed at the centre of the ambit; a focus placed at one of ,the extremities will give a unidirectional space. A curved space thus constituted can naturally have one or several focuses. *Regular spaces* will now be those which always adopt the same temperament whatever the module; they will be *irregular* in the opposite case. This variation of partition can be established in terms of a basic partition, in which case the irregular spaces will be focalised. They will be non-focalised in the opposite case. All the preceding observations of focuses in curved spaces are equally applicable here. The various categories—straight, curved, regular, irregular— refer to striated space. Smooth space can only be classified in a more general fashion, that is to say, by the statistical distribution of the frequencies found within it. If the distribution is more or less equal throughout the ambit, the space will be non-directed; there will be one or more pseudo-focuses when the distribution, being unequal, becomes denser and more constricted at one or more points. There is an ambiguity between smooth and striated space; a strongly directed smooth space tends to be confused with a striated space; inversely, a striated space in which the statistical distribution of the pitches used is *in fact* equal tends to be confused with a smooth space. Nevertheless, the definition can be found in the context, which throws into relief or annuls this ambiguity.

Finally, the following table is established:

I. *Homogeneous spaces*
  A. Striated spaces:
    1. Defined partition, fixed or variable
      (a) Fixed module: straight spaces
      (b) Variable module: curved spaces

       Focalised $\left\{ \begin{array}{l} \text{One focus} \\ \text{Several focuses} \end{array} \right.$

       Non-focalised

    2. Fixed or variable module
      (a) Fixed defined partition: regular spaces

(b) Variable defined partition: irregular spaces

Focalised $\left\{\begin{array}{l}\text{One focus}\\\text{Several focuses}\end{array}\right.$

Non-focalised

B. Smooth spaces:
    Undefined partition; no module
    Statistical distribution of frequencies:
       Equal: non-directed space
       Unequal: directed space—pseudo-focus(es)

II. *Non-homogeneous spaces*

Smooth/striated spaces $\left\{\begin{array}{l}\text{Alternation}\\\text{Superposition}\end{array}\right.$

It is evident that this table can be applied to time if tempo is included; this is because there are likewise two categories in musical time: *pulsed* time—the only term which seems to fit the description of the phenomenon to which I wish to relate it—and *amorphous* time. In *pulsed* time, the structures of duration will be related to chronometric time as landmarks, or, one might say, systematically placed regular or irregular beacons: these constitute a pulsation, either of the smallest unit (the smallest common multiple of all the values used), or of a simple multiple of this unit (two or three times its value). I have already mentioned that all values can, in practice, be reduced either to a single and regular pulsation, or to two unequal pulsations in the proportion of two to three; the exceptions are rare and result from a truncated division of the unit. *Amorphous* time is only related to chronometric time in a global sense; durations, whether with defined proportions (not values) or having no indication of proportion, appear in a field of time. Only pulsed time is susceptible to speed, acceleration or deceleration: the regular or irregular referential system on which it is based is a function of a chronometric time of greater or lesser delimitation, breadth or variability. The relationship of chronometric time to the number of pulsations will be the index of speed. Amorphous time can vary only in density according to the statistical number of events which take place during a chronometric global time-span; the relationship of this density or an amorphous time-span will be the index of content. Our previous comparison will illustrate these abstract ideas. Beneath a line of reference, place a *completely* smooth surface and a striated surface; it makes no difference whether the striation is regular or irregular. If this *ideal* smooth surface is displaced, it will give no indication of either the speed or the direction of its displacement, since there is no guidemark for the eye. The displacement of a striated surface will on the contrary be immediately notice-able, both in its speed and its direction. Amorphous time is comparable to the smooth surface, pulsated time to the striated surface; by analogy, I will call these two categories smooth time and striated time.

If our observations on pitch are to be applied to smooth and striated time, a few remarks on the practical implications of these concepts will first be necessary. Is it possible to *realise* smooth and striated spaces, and if so, *how*? The problem seems simple, in principle. It would be solved by the construction of instruments whose temperament could be precisely varied according to prepared and ordered combinations—a procedure comparable to the preparation of registrations on the modern organ. These instruments, by no means unimaginable or unrealisable, should be constructed from materials which are not sensitive to atmospheric variations of humidity, temper-ature, etc.; in other words, they should stay absolutely 'in tune'. Could 'natural' instruments ever fulfil this condition? In most cases this is very doubtful, and considering the difficulty of tuning certain instruments with sufficient accuracy to the tempered semitone one cannot hold out great hopes for similar instruments in the realm of finer differentiations; this is even more obvious if one imagines an ensemble of such instruments. Non-homogeneous spaces may well occur—this seems more than likely!—but they will be anything but control-lable. Ought *specialised* instruments to be used for certain types of realisation? The organ constructed by Professor Fokker[1]

[1] *Professor Fokker's organ:* a pipe organ constructed to an equal temper-ment of 31 notes to the octave, with the addition of a separate 12-note

according to Huyghens' temperament of the fifth of a tone points the way; one can imagine the effect of an organ whose stops will correspond not to particular timbres, but to different definitions of musical space. The keyboard—or any means of materialising the sound—would be the tablature giving varied interpretations of a single symbol. However, electronic vibrations remain the material most independent of atmospheric conditions, and this direction will have to be explored further if we are to find an instrument to correspond to these theoretical views on musical space. By means of a certain number of operations, it would certainly be possible to obtain nearly everything which is audible—and even more!—by partitioning the continuum in some way. Having a computer, able to memorise, record and realise all the possible combinations, this ideal instrument would be remarkably useful. We can imagine its theoretical realisation, but in practice, instrument-making is beset by considerable forces of inertia, which must be dealt with if one is not to be confined to writing music for the archives. The very great success of instruments like the xylophone, tubular bells, etc. arises largely from this nostalgia for relative space, which is empirically realised by means of instruments of complex spectra, evolving extensively according to dynamics and tessitura; the use of sound objects obtained from strongly contrasting instruments, with systematically antinomic modes of attack, likewise indicates this desire to go *beyond* tempered space, making use of the very qualities which most violently contradict its principle: the natural characteristics of the instruments are clearly opposed to any theoretically imposed division. This empirical research is extremely fruitful, because it means that due attention must be given to the generative potential of the musical material. But we should still aim for the practical realisation of instruments we consider indispensable to musical evolution.

If I have stressed the realisation of new musical spaces by

keyboard and pedalboard which—by means of coupling to the large organ —can select a number of different 12-note scales from the complete 31. Designed by Adrian Fokker, this organ was installed in Teyler's Museum at Haarlem in 1950. (Trans.)

instruments, electronic or not, it is because it seems extremely important not to abandon 'the realm of music' to mechanical electro-acoustic media alone. The latter, as already explained, will certainly be able, before long, to resolve many problems; they will, however, remain no less rigid prisoners of a fixed and definitive realisation. All in all, the future in this field does not really seem to depend on magnetic tape and the recording on it of sound phenomena created by specialised equipment; but—as two realisations in Munich and New York have shown —a more accurate view of things leads to a *codification* which uses systems of perforated cards or ribbons. The creation of an electronic sound world does not seem necessarily to entail artisan methods, whereas automation is ideally suited to this line of research. However this may be, instruments using a tablature and pure electro-acoustic procedures will provide all these musical spaces, which seem of prime importance, both at the present time and for the future.

The problem of duration is of the same order; apart from a fundamental difference between the two elements, pitch and duration. This difference is tempo. As I have already mentioned, the only non-tempered or non-homogeneous spaces which can be *easily* realised are due to chance alone, and are completely uncontrollable; these accidents of material or of performance cannot possibly be reckoned with. On the other hand, with duration, there are two ways of obtaining values in which the time proportion will be refined in relation to existing concepts: if certain sub-divisions can only be realised by the intervention of electro-mechanical procedures, others can be brought about by the interpreter and by the concept of tempo. In the first case, exact, determinate results will be obtained; in the second, the results occur within a variable field. Before developing this point, we must extend the comparison between smooth and striated time and space.

Pulsation is for striated time what temperament is for striated space; it has been shown that, depending on whether partition is fixed or variable, defined space will be regular or irregular; similarly, that the pulsation of striated time will be regular or irregular, but systematic. This pulsation is not realisable—either in execution or in conception—except when it observes relatively simple proportions; our study of duration-series showed that the succession or superposition of certain proportions would be unrealisable in practice, as for example when truncated, uneven divisions are interspersed with silences.[1] If the alternations of proportions are complex, precise and instantaneous—that is to say, discontinuous—or if the variations in pulsation are strict, only electro-mechanical means will be able to realise them with sufficient accuracy. Take an example: suppose I establish a logarithmic time scale within a value forming part of a general series (and not ordering the multiples of the unit, as is usually the case). If its structures are based on values of subdivisions, that is to say, those which do not follow each other in an increasing or decreasing order, they cannot be executed manually but only with the help of a mechanical control. The only sequences which can be approximately interpreted are those of an increasing or decreasing order. This involves a subterfuge, which consists in notating equal values, but varying the tempo; in other words, I divide the assessment of the value into two operations: I choose a single proportion in relation to the pulsation, and I alter the speed of this pulsation, so that its chronometric time evolves in the precise direction intended. I deliberately chose the simple example of the logarithmic scale, because it is very similar to an equal pulsation that is affected by a constant elementary dimension of tempo: accelerando or ritardando; but, from the dialectic between pulsation and pace, one can in effect *regain* all the possibilities of proportions which were left to the machine. It is sufficient, in fact, to conceive of irregular and irregularly subdivided pulsations—as long as they are realisable, that is to say, do not exceed a certain complexity of proportions and of divisions, already indicated—as being acted upon by all the possible envelopes of tempo: straight lines, broken lines, curved lines (in constant, irregular or fluctuating evolution). As soon as a chronometric value is envisaged bi-dimensionally or bi-functionally, a high degree of differentiation is obtained, although account must always be taken of the margin of

[1] See p. 52.

imprecision of the general nature of the field in which this differentiation exists. Thus, there is no fundamental difference between mechanical and human means of realising duration, as there is in the realisation of musical spaces, but a difference of degree in the precision and discontinuity of the operation. In fact, if the logarithmic scale is mechanically transcribed in all its permutations, it must, for realisation to be humanly possible, be inscribed in an enveloping curve. Compared with mechanically possible differentiations of duration, those available to the performer are, in the last analysis, limited by directed envelopes; in any case, what is lost in precision is gained in suppleness of articulation, an appreciable advantage in many cases.

With the help of these detailed particulars on the dialectics of relative tempo proportions we can proceed with the classification of time. *Straight time*, corresponding to straight space, will, whatever the partition, observe a constant module; in other words, the original values being comprised between two limits, the derived values will be comprised between the multiples of the relationship defined by these two limits. *Curved time*, on the contrary, will cause the derived values to depend upon a function of the relationship defined by these two limits (all the values will for example be augmented or diminished according to the direction of the time-register which is followed.) Whatever the module, *regular time* will be that in which partition remains fixed; *irregular*, where partition varies (according to a defined numerical proportion or to the tempo). *Smooth time* will have neither partition nor module; in the same way as with pitch, statistical distribution will give such time direction or non-direction. As before, curved or irregular striated time will be either focalised or non-focalised, one or more focuses ordering the partial or total symmetries. Similarly we shall have *homogeneous time*, whether exclusively smooth or striated; and *non-homogeneous time*, where striated and smooth time will alternate or be superposed. Again, as with pitch, the ambiguity between smooth and striated becomes evident in the disposition of durations, which are susceptible to two interpretations. Whether it belongs to one or the other of these categories, time is, according to the distribution of durations, either directional or non-directional; but a static distribution in striated time will tend to give the impression of smooth time, whereas a differentiated and *directed* distribution in smooth time, especially when based on adjacent values, may easily be confused with the usual results of striated time.

One of the consequences of this ambiguity may be currently observed when proportional time notation is abandoned, in favour of giving note-values in chronometric bars—in seconds. What happens then? The performer, instead of producing smooth time, will automatically return to striated time, where the unit of reference will be the second—he will fall back on the metronomic unit equal to 60; this confirms how false and illusory directly chronometric notation is in most cases, since the result will directly contradict the intention. True smooth time is that over which the performer has no control. A particular case will make this clearer; suppose that a group of instruments is playing in striated time, under a conductor, and that two instruments have to play, within a global smooth time, structures whose time is partly smooth and partly striated, though differently from that of the group. By the very fact of this alternation, the two instrumentalists will lose all sense of the regular striated time which accompanies them and they are thus necessarily placed in a smooth global time. Certain irregular signs from the conductor will, in addition, discourage all inclination towards striated time. This example is intended to show that smooth time is a much more subtle organisation than a simple chronometry expressed in seconds; the latter leads, finally, to elementary striated time, except when an instrument of measurement, the chronometer, is used. Only then can complete independence be attained, since participation in both operations—counting time and 'filling' it—is no longer necessary. This brings me to a definition of the operations which constitute smooth and striated time: in smooth time, time is filled without counting; in striated time, time is filled by counting. These two relationships seem to me of prime importance in the theoretical and practical evaluation of temporal structures; they are the fundamental laws of time in music.

Lastly, remember that in the classification we have just established, the concepts of continuity and discontinuity are again linked by *partition;* the variability of the unit of partition will be obtained either directly (any partition whatsoever—an even or uneven division of the unit, used in any proportion—is always mechanically possible), or by the alternation of tempo (approximate values); when the interval of partition tends towards the epsilon of perception, discontinuity merges into continuity.

The worlds of timbre and amplitude are not so easily dealt with. Curiously enough, their customary use is based on exactly opposite characteristics; timbre is currently used in a discontinuous manner, apart from certain exceptional experiments in ambiguity with instrumental groups, while dynamics as a rule resorts to a continuous gesture. One of the greatest difficulties met with in the interpretation of contemporary music is the realisation of a discontinuous dynamic, which, until now, has been limited to *subito sforzando* or *piano subito.* However, in these two domains, it is impossible to observe the same strictness as in pitch and duration. On the one hand, the organisation of timbre will not admit of the concept of partition previously established; when working with frequencies or durations—and even with amplitude measured electro-acoustically—one is working with simple, linear data, whereas, timbre being a complex function of pitch, duration and amplitude, a continuum of timbre entails that of the complex function itself. Amplitude, on the other hand, has in musical practice a much more restricted ambit than the three other properties of sound, and, except in the case of control by means of a measuring apparatus, partition can only be precise if it is sufficiently broad; limited both in its ambit and by the natural restrictions of partition, the domain of amplitude is not susceptible to so great a diversity of means. The customary use of timbre and amplitude only serves to mirror the profound laws which govern their existence.

Bearing in mind the limitations and inadequacies of such a 'transcription', the terms 'smooth' and 'striated' can be adapted to the complexity of timbre and restricted to the narrow scope of amplitude: above all, the dialectic of continuity and discontinuity remains. Concerning timbre, the module can be a given succession of timbres or groups of timbres, forming a period; by analogy, the partition will be each element or group of elements of which this period is constituted; the focus will thus be defined as a single family, composed of similar timbres. With the help of this adaptation, the broad categories of striated and smooth space are applicable to timbre. By timbre, I mean of course not only the spectrum itself, but also the processes involved in attack, suspension and release, from which the evolution of the spectrum is inseparable; in other words, timbre is not to be considered in its static aspect alone, but also kinematically. With regard to amplitude, a simple dimension, the table can remain unaltered, but, as already indicated, everything will take place in a restricted ambit: the variability of the module could not be more limited, especially as far as instruments are concerned, in music for soloists; with a large group of instruments, one can exploit the density, and the difference of dynamic scales particular to each instrument, thus considerably enlarging the ambit. In electro-acoustic music, the problem is naturally presented in other terms, since proportions are established which can, by amplification, be transcribed at will up to the power-limit of the means of transmission. The results obtained by amplification in a circuit of loud-speakers can be obtained instrumentally—broadly speaking, of course—by a large group of instruments having strongly differentiated dynamic scales. Thus, the duality we observed between absolute proportions and tessitura, between numerical durational porportions and tempo, appears once more in the field of amplitude: in the case of electro-acoustic transmissions, amplitude has the precision of absolute proportions and tessitura (measurable in decibels); in the case of a group of instruments, the relative global amplitude—the general tessitura—is a function of the relative individual amplitude—a partial tessitura.

With regard to true space, which is, as we have seen, a distribution of structures and a function of the four components, it is necessary to adopt the same definition as for timbre: the module will be the conjunction of a periodic distance with the periodicity of the elements, or groups of elements, inscribed within it. Partition will be the division of this distance corresponding to an element or group of elements of the period; the focus will be defined as a point or surface, coupled with a specific family of phenomena.

Before tackling syntax itself we must deal with the word proportion; in fact, we have contrasted proportions (of frequencies, for example)—that is to say, geometrical progressions—with arithmetical progressions (above all, those of durations); in particular, the former have been defined as having no functional relationship with the latter. This is somewhat precipitate, and overlooks the definition of geometrical and arithmetical progressions and the part played by logarithms. Logarithms are defined as the terms of an arithmetical progression beginning at zero which correspond in rank to terms of a geometrical progression beginning with the unit; thus, by logarithm, a geometrical progression will correspond to an arithmetical one. This relation is involved whenever we speak of pitches as intervals or as frequency relationships. A fourth can be defined just as easily by an arithmetical progression—the octave less a fifth—as by a geometrical progression—$2 \times 2/3 = 4/3$. Likewise two semitones make a tone, two tones a major third, etc., by addition; in order to obtain the frequency ratio of a third, I multiply the ratios of the two seconds by each other. Conversely, the addition of frequencies results in a logarithmic scale of intervals; the sequence of frequencies: 40–80–120, etc., yields the sequence of intervals: octave, fifth, fourth, etc. Similarly, with durations, the multiplication of the unit by each whole number in turn will result in an arithmetical progression (Ex. 11); but the progressive multiplication of each multiple of the unit by a single whole number will result in a geometrical progression.

A geometrical progression will result if the unit is divided by each whole number in turn (Ex. 12); but, within a given division, there will be an arithmetical progression from the submultiple to the unit.

97

Ex. 37

♪ ♩ ♩ ○ *etc.*

Ex. 38

1:5	2:5	3:5	4:5	Unit
♪	♩	♩.	♩	♩

Instead of superficially denying the existence of a function between arithmetical and geometrical progressions, it is necessary to emphasise that their relationship is, on the contrary, one of the principal functions of musical constituents. This is why a geometrical series may very well be transcribed as an arithmetical series, in other words, proportional relationships as intervallic addition and vice versa, by means of logarithms. This will make it possible to proceed from frequencies to durations and vice versa, with extreme suppleness and complete justification. It is no less interesting to mix the two progressions; to inscribe arithmetical progressions between the terms of a geometrical progression, or vice versa —one might even say 'between' or 'starting from'. In the case of pitch, for example, this will result in harmonic series on a given frequency, which can be used in the field of resonances, or in the writing of 'mutations'; in the case of duration, it will lead to fractions of multiples of the unit.

I have developed this idea, first of all because it seems important in a theoretical process which aims to unify and to synthesise the various domains of sound; secondly, because certain superficial objections have long called for a refutation. Strict reasoning and precise definition seem indispensable steps towards meaningful speculation. I have pointed out the confusion between period and phase, two terms which nevertheless have perfectly established scientific definitions; even less understandable, muscular energy has been confused with the speed of free fall; hence my insistence upon accuracy in morphological definitions. Now that the principle of serialism and the zones in which it operates have been examined, we reach the third stage: how are these various zones organised amongst themselves according to the serial principle? This leads us to the logic of *relationships*.

MUSICAL SYNTAX

In the course of this study, we have sketched out the relationships which can exist between the various serial functions. It should be specified, however, that the series possesses intrinsic characteristics. These depend, as we have seen, on its very structure, the isomorphic figures which it contains, the symmetries which it includes and, in consequence, the selective powers which it possesses. But now it should be noted that series are organised between themselves according to their extrinsic characters; these are of two sorts, depending on criteria which we call criteria of definition or of selection, and criteria of combination or of arrangement. Before explaining these various points in detail, we must return to the *play* of serial structures in relation to each other.

It has already been indicated that the relationships between pitch and duration are established from simple to simple, simple to complex, complex to complex; but between pitch and duration on the one hand, dynamics and timbre on the other, they may also be established from simple to ensemble, from simple to ensemble of ensembles, from complex to ensemble, from complex to ensemble of ensembles. At the beginning of this chapter, it was also stated that interaction or interdependence functions as a vectorial compound, and that there could be either a principal (or primordial) organisation, with secondary (or supplementary) organisations, or a global organisation, which takes account of the various categories, without neglecting the intermediary levels of predominance of certain organisations in relation to others.

It is this last point which we will consider first. It would surely be illusory to try to link all the general structures of a work to one and the same global generative structure, from which they would necessarily derive in order to assure the cohesion and unity, as well as the uniquity of the work. This cohesion and uniquity cannot, in my opinion, be obtained so mechanically; the principle of allegiance of structures to a central authority seems rather to resort to Newtonian 'models', contradicting the developments of present-day thought.

Moreover, the problem is not new; it had already confronted an earlier generation in connection with the pitch series. Schoenberg implicitly admitted that a single series should be responsible for an entire work—whatever its duration, its importance and the diversity of its 'incidents'; even if he did not draw up this method in principle, he always practised it, and his disciples did not fail to transform this general idea into a golden rule. Webern, the proportions of whose works were always somewhat limited, obeyed the same law: the uniquity of the basic series. Nevertheless, as his *Second Cantata* so strikingly demonstrates, he strove more and more to base each section of a work on specific characteristics, to the exclusion of all other possibilities contained in the series. His selective organisation of *limited serial ensembles* depends on true serial functions, that is to say, on privileged regions and the relationships consequent upon them; this selection is also based on the linking functions of privileged regions found at the extremes of the series. In the *Second Cantata* for example, the first movement uses only two series, while the second 'consumes' the twenty-four transpositions (original and inversion). Webern originated the extremely fruitful idea of taking the series as a factor of unification of sub- and super-groups. In effect, all the isomorphic figures found in the basic structures are dependent on the fact that they always succeed one another in the same order, according to the given transpositions and inversions; they are integrated into the chromatic complement, a condition *sine qua non* of the series of twelve semitones. These isomorphic figures are the basis of privileged ensembles which reproduce on a higher level the part which they play within the series; the ensemble obtained by the linking of series having specific privileges becomes in itself a kind of superior series. The series itself can thus be considered as the structural power of *mediation* between sub- and super-groups. Berg, for his part, clearly understood the advantages of not limiting himself to the use of a single series, even though its various forms might be selected and grouped into limited ensembles; already embryonic in a scene from *Wozzeck* (the Passacaglia of Act I), this idea of deriving other forms from the

100

original series to obtain new characteristics constantly occupied him thereafter. In the third movement of the *Lyric Suite*, the series of the first movement acquires a different personality by means of an exchange within the order of the notes; this personality is again transformed in the fifth movement, as a result of two additional exchanges. In *Lulu*, Berg creates from the basic series a group of derived series, intended to characterise persons or situations. This is achieved by various methods, such as the return to a dissimilar horizontal of vertical forms derived from the horizontal original, permutations obtained by regular extrapolation of notes. Berg's gesture, even in the *Lyric Suite*, is as dramatic as it is organic; his serial derivations generally, and above all in *Lulu*, lead to strongly contrasted thematic organisms.

The personalities of Schoenberg, Webern and Berg have thus shown the different angles from which the serial function can be regarded in relation to the organisation of a work. Nevertheless, they always depended on a basic ensemble, implicit or explicit, of the four-times-twelve fundamental forms of the series. Whatever their attitude to the specified or unique qualities of the serial form being used, they always kept to one of these forms. In addition, it is well known that—with the occasional exception of Berg—the idea of circular permutation acting on a series did not occur to them, nor did it coincide with their conception; for them, the overall ensemble was formed from series whose beginnings and ends could never vary—hence the extreme importance accorded by Webern to the functions of linking.

The same problems exist today in more general terms:

1. Should a single organisation govern the ensemble of components?
2. Equally, should no more than a single organisation govern each individually conceived component?

With regard to the ensemble of components, any form of reasoning which consists in justifying a unique organisation by the unique character of a given work is hardly satisfactory. It reverts to Schoenbergian practice at its most unimaginative, if the method which it implies is strictly followed. To speak of a specific organisation reserved solely for a specific work seems to me to show ignorance of the law of large numbers, and consequently to depend on a quite Utopian concept. Starting from similar basic elements, how can the derived complexes fail to be grouped into a family of relationships, according to certain archetypes? The same *objects* may not be found in the course of two different works, but they will be of the same nature; and, in this sense, if the combinations are limitless, the categories are far from being so. We can no longer pretend that our perceptions are capable of reducing the various sound phenomena such as pitch and duration to common patterns; in particular, recent experiences would seem to prove the inadequacy of the law of Weber-Fechner; musical practice, after all, proves that durations are not 'gauged' in the same way as intervals, however well-trained the ear. Again, it is a question of the categories which are perceived with the maximum acuity. If two durations do not observe a simple relationship and are not part of a figure or a repeated metre which thus 'counts' for us, their comparison necessitates counting the time by means of a chosen standard—whether it be the second or some other appropriate unit. Those with absolute pitch have no need of a point of reference for the direct evaluation of a frequency; it will be estimated to the nearest semitone, if the intervals are non-tempered. The matter becomes more delicate with micro-intervals, especially when they are of minute proportions. Different traditions attach different degrees of importance to the education of duration perception; an Indian will probably have a greater aural finesse in the estimation of time, just as he shows a superiority in the evaluation of small intervals. However, I have yet to meet a musician having a 'perfect ear', from the point of view of duration, to say nothing of tempo and dynamics. If timbres are almost instantly recognisable—except in certain short and complex combinations—it is because they are presented as organised emsembles, and because the individuality of pure timbres, as far as instruments are concerned, can easily be remembered since these are few in number. Taking into account the true

complexity of perception, one cannot say that a single organisation will respond better to its needs than multiple organisations;
this single organisation will, perhaps, be a more intellectually
attractive hypothesis, although tastes vary, but it would be
vain to justify it otherwise.

The single organisation will be considered as a special case,
not excluding others; this will, so to speak, prolong the
Schoenbergian use of the series. We can equally well conceive of
Webernian and Bergian prolongations. I use these terms with
reference to the cases previously explained; but, in order
to avoid all confusion, I will set out the three types of serial
usage in any given work as follows:

— Uniquity of the serial hierarchy; fixed typology and
characterology (Schoenberg).

— Uniquity of the series; selectivity due to the internal
structural characteristics (Webern).

— (One or more) multiform series of varying typology and
characterology (Berg).

The first type has already been explained; the second offers
more varied possibilities. To each of the sound components of a
fundamental series, we will attribute an ensemble selected by
common characteristics; each component will be linked to a
central organising factor, but will exist through its own
characteristics; thus, in each domain, we ought to envisage a
sub-ensemble rather than an ensemble of properties. Extending
the concept mentioned earlier on the subject of Webern's
pitch series, the series may be considered as a structural
power of mediation between the sub- and super-ensembles.
Selectivity will confer special functions on each sound component, which will be free to 'envelop' the others just as much
as it may be ordered by them, according to the selective force
displayed by each in relation to the other. Such interplay
of equilibrium will only really take place in structures organised
in this way; this is some measure of its usefulness.

The third type of relationship is much more complex and a
complete exploration of this field necessitates a deviation from
Berg's original thought. In this type, we can establish a

fundamental series, structurally concerned with one component, its transformations being related to the other components. There will no longer be a 'balance', or shifting emphasis on the importance of different organisations; instead there will be an antagonism of divergent functions, some subduing the others. An extension of this principle will result in series that obey completely different organisational criteria, initially linked, however, by structural parallelisms, or even by what may be called *accidents* of positioning. By this, I mean that the divergent organisms will have been linked in the *original* figures by relationships which will be respected throughout the work. It is unnecessary to specify the parallelism of the structures, whether evident in the shape, the organisation or the repetition of series.

Having defined the three types of organisation which govern the relations of the four components, we must now consider each domain in particular, where, naturally, all three types will recur. They can be interlinked by means of a new concept, global and local structuration, which I propose to explain. It is hardly necessary to say that a referential hierarchy is required to define a given work, if not in its entirety, at least in its principal events. A generalised series is indispensable to the creation of elementary morphologies, the first plans of development, but it ought not to remain the only reference in the course of composition; this basic series will enable us to formulate objects which, in their turn, can be the basis of serial generation. Thus, to each original object will correspond a specific development organised according to its own intrinsic qualities: this will lead directly to the use of defective or limited series as defined above, in short, to the use of the various sub-ensembles dependent on a given ensemble. This 'deployment' of local structures has supplanted thematic development, and hence is of supreme importance. It is a question of practising a selective operation, concerning only the one structure directly involved. Thus, a specific development, organically linked to the larger basic structure, is continually being created. In this way, a justified freedom is achieved, the essential decisions being left to the momentary initiative of the composer.

His imagination is free to work on the concrete object which arises in the course of composition, and to do this in terms of the object itself. In comparison with the practice of Webern or Berg, we are no longer dealing with serial ensembles but with partial, local structures, having their own independence, while retaining their filiation with the global structure. A global structure will create a cascade of local structures directly dependent on itself. This is a structural technique comparable to series-connection or parallel connection in electrical wiring.

Since the functions of the different serial structures need not remain closely parallel, but may, to a certain extent, affirm their independence from one another—they may be established as already mentioned, from point to point, from point to ensemble, etc.—it is essential to discover to what extent we can make a transition from strict to free writing. This distinction —a constant of music—is now expressed in other terms: unique form of existence, and indeterminate probability. If I may resort to a comparison (but only a *comparison*), a point is defined by the intersection of two lines, a line by the intersection of two planes, and a plane by the intersection of two volumes; in a volume, there will be an infinity of planes, in a plane, an infinity of lines and in a line, an infinity of points. This reminder of elementary geometry is only meant to suggest the interaction between two, three or four components. When a structure coincides with all others at a given point, this point is *unique* and thus *binding*; the more the field of encounter is enlarged, the more numerous the possibilities and the more various the solutions: by means of this expedient the polyvalency of the structures can be re-established. More explicitly, if at each point all the components are renewed, we will obtain only *binding* and absolutely defined points: this is the extreme of strict writing, which is only possible when series are 'pre-controlled', with a definite end in view; otherwise, the 'ballistics' of sound will intervene, resulting in absurdities. If all the components *but one* are renewed, all the sound phenomena will be produced on a given line, defined by the invariable component; if all the components *but two* are renewed, the phenomena will be produced in a plane defined by the invariable components;

and so on. A progressive loosening of the vice-like grip of strict writing will finally lead to complete freedom—freedom, of course, within general structural principles. At the point where all organisations are synchronised, there will be no freedom of choice, probability having entered into the structures themselves; when none of the organisations is synchronised, I can choose one of the possibilities offered, or avoid choosing altogether, making it the performer's responsibility: probability returns, but now it directs the structures from outside. Let it be clear that rigour and automatism in the meeting of structures lead to the same aesthetic result as freedom and choice. This leads us directly to the use of polyvalent forms and to the intervention of probability; we will return to this problem in the chapter devoted to aesthetics and poetics, but it is mentioned here in order to show that it is based in morphology itself and therefore is not an alien property that is grafted on along the way, or in the course of the form, to put it more precisely. The play of structures implicitly suggests a scale of relationships going from the chance of automatism to the chance of choice, taking in the fixed types that we already know. Perhaps we are only being wise after the event, and perhaps reflections on form have themselves initiated the search for polyvalent forms; but the hierarchy must be re-established in its true perspective: morphology can be held responsible for the abolition of fixity in musical structures.

We ought now to study the criteria within a work's organisation responsible for the ordering of the series, starting with the criteria of definition or of selection. These are, of course, extrinsic characteristics, and must not be confused with the true structural criteria which define the series. This selection is made according to extremely simple norms, which will be self-explanatory:

1. Repose or fixity
2. Movement or change

and of course these norms apply to various aspects of the organisations of the sound phenomenon; particular cases will be examined.

Fixity or change play their part in the various stages of morphology or of syntax, and are not obligatorily homogeneous: an examination of their processes will clarify their functions. The criteria of selection are first applied to an elementary organism, or to a specific ensemble of elementary organisms, already constituted; but they can be applied equally well to the very functions of constitution. In the first case, the selection groups together constituted organisms of the same nature and is therefore homogeneous—even more so when it only applies to a single organism; this will not be the case when the functions of constitution are governed by fixity or change, because fixity and change can be made to concern different functions: the selection will be non-homogeneous, in other words, half fixed and half mobile. Take pitch as an example, always bearing in mind that a pitch is analysed according to its *absolute* place in a serial function, and according to its *actual* place in the dispositions of tessitura. We will take a single series of twelve notes, *a*, grouped into several dissimilar figures:

Ex. 39

for the moment, this will be considered as an absolute model.

If this series alone is used, the maximum degree of structural repose will result, since the succession of intervals will return periodically and remain absolutely unchanged. Add to this series a new series, *b*, a transposition of the first, differently grouped (Ex. 39); when the order *ab*, *ab*, etc. is constantly employed, the field of fixity will have been enlarged by introducing a succession of intevals which are different, but equally invariable: mobility will nevertheless intervene in this fixed field, if the order of succession is altered to a form of the type: *ab*, *ba*, *ba*, *ab*, etc. Clearly, the larger the field of fixity, the greater the mobility, since the possibility of permutating selected elements will increase. The field can also be conceived as mobile: selection within it will be mobile, but it can, however, tend towards to fixity. Suppose that the mobile field proceeds from series *a* used alone, to the succession *a*, *b*, *c*; if, whatever the field (*a*, *ab*, *bc*, *abd*) the series is always used in the order: *a*, *b*, *c*, it is clear that the same succession of intervals or the same sequence of relationships will tend to result; the orientation towards fixity will be indicated by the greater or lesser number of elements common to the mobile fields. Finally, in the extreme case of mobility, there will be no field at all, and the choice will fall indiscriminately on this or that structure; only variations in the frequency of the return of given elements will occur, and these will create virtual fields of fixity. The variations of the field are summarised in Table 1. Let us take another concrete example. If series *a* and *b* are analysed solely with regard to pitch, it is clear that they have the same provenance, since *b* is the transposition of *a* at the augmented fourth; however, the grouping has undergone an evolution between them: the first adheres to the scheme 1–3/1/ 2–2–3, the second to 3/1–3–1/2–2. A transformation has taken place; this transformation could, moreover, have been brought to bear on a characteristic other than the grouping: density, for example. If, corresponding to series *a*, we have series *A*, 'enriched' as a function of its groupings, the transformation by density is mobile; if we have a corresponding series *A'*, uniformly 'enriched', the transformation by density is fixed (Ex. 39). Whether passing from *a* to *b*, to *A* or to *A'*, the generative process is identical; only the characteristics of the transformation evolve. This generative process, however,

108

TABLE 1

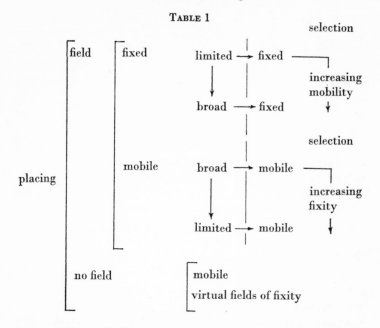

can equally well be considered as varying, when different methods of serial deduction are employed in passing from one series to another (a single series to a series of chords, for example). These observations apply to the internal structure of the series, but the criteria of selection may apply equally well to the presentation, or external structure; they will determine, so to speak, the *modes of description* of a series. Series A (Ex. 39), consists of sound blocks of unequal density, to which a single mode of description may be applied, for instance an upward arpeggio or simultaneous attack (Ex. 40a, b); in this case, there will be fixity of the external structure. Its mobility implies different descriptions of blocks which could be specified as in Ex. 40c.

In the first section, with the grouping 1–3, the upward arpeggio will be applied to the isolated block, the downward arpeggio to the three other blocks; the second section is composed of a single sound, which annuls all group description (it could be related to the other blocks by dynamic description,

109

Ex. 40a–c

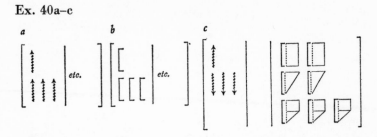

but here we are only concerned with pitches); in the third section, with grouping 2–2–3, simultaneous attack and release will be applied to the two first notes, simultaneous attack and successive release to the next two, and simultaneous attack and half simultaneous, half successive release to the last three.

The selective criteria of internal and external structures may be summarised as in Table 2.

Each table represents a clearly determined function: the *placing* operates on constituted ensembles, and indicates their order of employment, independently of the characteristics of the series itself or of its derivatives; the *production*, on the other hand, concerns their internal and external structure. These

TABLE 2

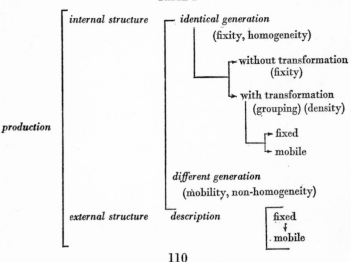

110

two sets of operations define all the trajectories which lead from fixity to mobility. A study of this table will show that they are innumerable; the imagination is almost at a loss, and finds it difficult to take in all the possibilities offered by this aspect of serial structure—possibilities which the imagination must nevertheless learn to control. Again, we have not considered pitch other than as an absolute phenomenon; tessitura enriches this field and leads to the independent play of its own structures. It too can evolve from total fixity to total mobility, the index of fixity covering a more or less restricted field. The *index of fixity* is the ratio between the number of fixed frequencies and that of mobile or semi-mobile frequencies (whether an absolute pitch has its tessitura renewed on each of its appearances, or whether the tessitura changes regularly or irregularly after one or more appearances). The field of fixity may be explained thus: when the fixity is concerned with the same absolute pitches (whatever the index), the field will be null; it will be enlarged progressively as fixity is displaced and attains a greater number of absolute pitches different from those preceding it; the field will be extended to its maximum when the displacement of fixity *'paralyses'* entirely new elements. These functions of tessitura can maintain direct organic relationships with the serial functions, and can, as a result, corroborate them; but they can also be completely independent, mechanically applied, and can impose their own outline pattern, and thus tend to 'erase' or erode the serial

TABLE 3

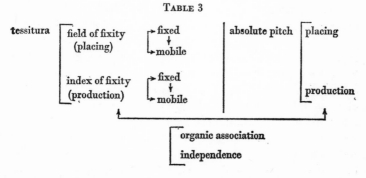

functions. The following table corresponds to the selection of tessitura, and is to be seen as parallel with that already established for absolute pitch. (Table 3.)

In order to clarify the ideas which we have just developed, let us take another example. Series *A* (Ex. 39), is an 'enriched' series corresponding to series *a*. Suppose I should want to *bring out* structure *a* within *A* by means of tessitura; to do this, I must isolate the individual tessituras of *a*. There are two solutions: to give a fixed tessitura to the notes of *a* in all the appearances of *A*, and to attribute a mobile tessitura to the complementary notes of each block; or else to give a mobile tessitura to the notes of *a*, while attributing a fixed tessitura to the complementary notes. The first solution is shown in Ex. 41a.

Ex. 41a–b

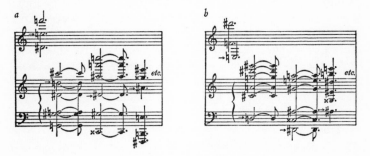

A comparison of Ex. 39a with Ex. 41a will show that the notes E♮ D♮ D♯ A♯ remain in the same position (these are the notes of *a*), but that all the other notes in each block have changed register; the relationship common to Ex. 39a and Ex. 41a will thus be *positively* displayed by the fixity of structure *a*. When comparing Ex. 39a and Ex. 41b, we note the opposite—figure *a* is mobile, the complementary blocks are fixed; the relationship is realised *negatively*. This example shows the organic liaison between a structure and the organisation of its tessituras. If the tessituras of structure *A* are varied, there will be a choice between: keeping structure *a* fixed (Ex. 42a), making it mobile (Ex. 42b)—the complementary sounds being seen respectively as mobile and fixed—and leaving structure *a* and its complementary sounds undifferentiated in mobility (Ex. 42c).

Ex. 42a–c

Another type of organic relationship can be shown, this time within series *A* (Ex. 39): considering the grouping of blocks 1–3, in the last three blocks we will fix the tessitura of the notes which constitute the first block: F♮, E♮, D♯. Thus, within the three mobile chords, the whole or a part of the fixed image—the 'spectre' of the first chord—will be found. There again, the relationship is *positive*. In the three blocks, the notes D♯; D♯ and E♮; D♯, E♮ and E♯ are marked with arrows.

Ex. 43

An opposite or negative relationship can easily be imagined. Finally there is a type of non-organic relationship; suppose that the general tessitura is fixed at four determined points: D♯ G♮ D♮ G♯, independently of the structure to which it is applied; these fixed, *non-structural* notes are conspicuous in each chord, respectively: D♯; D♯ G♮ D♮ G♯; D♯ C𝄪 G♯; D♯. Structure *a* is not thrown into relief within *A*,

113

8

nor is the physiognomy of the first block revealed in the three others: the internal and external structural characteristics of *A* are forced to disappear, or are at least strongly eroded, by being placed in conflict with a structure of inorganic tessitura.

Ex. 44

I have systematically described all these operations, but their usefulness will obviously increase with more supple applications: they serve to endow the embryonic organisms with personality, and are ostensibly the most indispensable and active auxiliaries of the work of organisation, of *composition*. Structures which have so far been considered as abstract networks of possibilities, now appear as precise figures, soon to become direct agents of the form. In order to reach this defined state, the criteria of selection will be generalised to cover all the structural domains: (a) *duration*, considered as actual value-relationships, in their tessitura and in their relationships with chronometric time; (b) *dynamics* seen from three aspects, subordinate dynamics, global dynamics and dynamic 'profile' (attack—suspension—release); (c) *timbre*. In addition, we must remember that spatial distribution is susceptible to the same criteria of repose or of movement. Once again, the table for pitch cannot be transcribed *literally* for the other structures: but at all costs, the categories of *placing* and of *production* must be retained. The necessary adaptations have already been explained with regard to other data, and it seems pointless to dwell on them here.

To conclude, the criteria of selection—fixity and mobility—will be applied to the general ensemble:

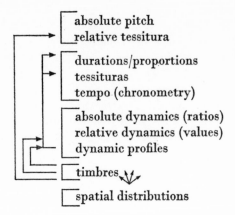

absolute pitch
relative tessitura

durations/proportions
tessituras
tempo (chronometry)

absolute dynamics (ratios)
relative dynamics (values)
dynamic profiles

timbres

spatial distributions

Timbre, of course, depends on relative tessituras, on general dynamics and on dynamic profile, and dynamic profile is closely linked to duration, while spatial distribution is a function of the four other categories. There is no need to describe the ensemble of constellations created by fixity and mobility; we shall merely draw attention to the immense *crescendo* leading from repose in all the organisations to movement in all the organisations, from the strictest order to a new reign of chaos.

Our next preoccupation must be the criteria of combination or of arrangement of serial organisms, in other words the syntactic organisation of the language. The forms of syntactic organisation are simple: monody, heterophony, polyphony; but they can equally well have recourse to complex concepts: polyphony of polyphonies, heterophony of heterophonies, heterophony of polyphonies, etc., by means of which simple forms are combined. Their definition has sometimes been problematic, due to associations with past forms of writing; even if the name subsists, the domain will sometimes be considerably enlarged. Rather than considering them in their historical context, the criteria of combination should be rationally classified, according to simple principles that can be reduced to two categories.

115

First, we will consider the *dimension* in which the events are produced. This dimension evolves from the horizontal to the vertical, with an intermediary, diagonal stage; it must again be stressed that these dimensions consist of one and the same characteristic modified by the internal time which rules the organisations and passes from zero (vertical, simultaneous) to a determinate number (horizontal, successive). Secondly, this classification will be founded on the *individual* or *collective* application of the structures. Using these two terms, all the combinatory phenomena of composition can be classified, on the level of elementary structures.

Monody will belong to the *horizontal-individual* order and homophony to the *horizontal-collective*. Though the characteristics of monody need hardly be described, it is as well to remember what is meant by homophony, in order to avoid any misunderstanding. Until now, this word has been used to characterise syllabic polyphonies (where all the voices coincide vertically on each syllable), as opposed to the contrapuntal style (where the voices are independent from a syllabic point of view). In this sense, homophony is the exclusively vertical and synchronous expression of polyphony, wherein harmonic functions have their part to play. But from now on, homophony can be considered as the direct transformation-by-density of monody—still regarded as unitary; this density, not being concerned with harmonic functions, will have its own structural principles, giving rise to fixed or variable homophonies. The following example is, in my opinion, very typical of one sort of homophony:

Ex. 45

This shows a single dimension: the structure sets out its objects horizontally, and the vertical density of each object is variable.

This is an example of vertical multiplication, but I could just as well have chosen a horizontal multiplication, the effect produced being comparable to a sort of echo or pre-echo of the monodic structure:

Ex. 46

From this example, it will be clear that I regard the domain of homophony as extraordinarily broad, so long as it depends on *horizontal-collective* criteria, however simple or complex its *appearance*.

The order *horizontal/diagonal/vertical—collective/individual* will define heterophony. As with homophony, the past use of the term must now be broadened and generalised. Heterophony can be defined, generally speaking, as the superposition on a primary structure of a modified *aspect* of the same structure; this should not be confused with polyphony, which makes a structure *responsible* for a new structure. In heterophony, several aspects of a fundamental formulation coincide (examples are found above all in the music of the Far East, where a very ornate instrumental melody is heterophonous with a

117

much more sober basic vocal line); its density will consist of various strata, rather as if several sheets of glass were to be superposed, each one bearing a variation of the same pattern. The basic dimension proceeds from the horizontal to the vertical (succession of one-dimensional figures, distribution of complex structures); this method of combination will derive a collectivity of structures from an individual model. Later we shall take heterophony as an example of syntactic transformation and all its possibilities will then be examined in detail.

We have considered in turn monody, homophony and heterophony; we must now study the concept of polyphony, which is distinguished, as I said, by the *responsibility* which it implies from one structure to another. Polyphony is based, in my opinion, on a fitting together of structures, which amounts to the use of 'counterpoint' and 'harmony', provided that the sense generally implied by these words is extended; or again, on a distribution such as can be related neither to harmony nor to counterpoint.

We will make the usual distinction between strict and free counterpoint; it will be free when the derived structures have only to comply with certain general norms; in the horizontal dimension, of course, the individual structure will be answerable only to the *collectivity* of the structures. Strict counterpoint, on the other hand, will demand exact correspondences between one structure or family of structures and another; and individual structure or ensemble will be individually answerable to the structure or the ensemble thus determined. The word structure, not figure, is intentionally used, because counterpoint can, in general horizontal relations, govern single figures as well as complex phenomena. Free counterpoint will, as a result, correspond to the order *horizontal-individual/collective*, strict counterpoint to the order *horizontal-individual/individual*.

If it depends directly on the figures implied by the series, harmony will be functional and will embrace the collectivity of vertical relationships; when it is not functional and is subject to such accidents as grouping, each relationship or group of relationships will obey individual criteria. Finally, if harmony, whatever its nature, is linked with new functions of density (fixed or variable) in order to produce 'mutations', the totality of relationships (functional, or having individual criteria) will be modified individually. As with counterpoint, any vertical relationship of points, figures or structures, can be considered as harmony.

Polyphony can also be described as the diagonal distribution of structures: 'parts' or 'voices', no longer exist, strictly speaking: the organisms are to be analysed as distributed structures; a morphological example in the organisation of a durational block was given earlier (Ex. 17). Syntactically, diagonal distribution acts individually or collectively on the individual figures and the collective ensembles of the structures.

Antiphony has not been mentioned, because it is a *distribution* of already 'formulated' polyphonic structures, and not a

TABLE 4

monody	horizontal	individual
homophony	horizontal	collective
heterophony	horizontal ↓ diagonal ↓ vertical	collective ← individual
polyphony (a) arrangement		
free counterpoint	horizontal	individual → collective
strict counterpoint	horizontal	individual ⇄ individual
functional harmony	vertical	collective
non-functional harmony	vertical	individual
multiplied harmony	vertical	individual → collective / individual
(b) distribution	diagonal	individual/collective ↓ individual/ collective

119

criterion of combination that might itself create a 'formulation'. Antiphony is already a formal prototype.

The criteria of combination are summarised in Table 4.

The isolation of each form of syntactic organisation remains a possibility and the advantages of manoeuvring homogeneous organisms from this point of view will be obvious; there is, however, an extra richness to be found in giving full rein to the cross-influences of the various criteria. It is possible not only to *combine* them, but also to *pass* from one to the other, that is to say, a monody can represent a 'reduced' polyphony, just as polyphony can be the distribution, the 'dispersion', of a monody. These structural illustrations will be explained further on.

First of all, and even before seeing how an organised world of sound can be built up from one of these basic criteria, the uniformity of our classification must be stressed. Monorhythm and homorhythm, heterorhythm and polyrhythm can be added as parallels to the terms already used; these will simply be the manifestation in terms of duration of the functions implicit in their correlatives. There can be no divergence, in this case; at the very most, there may be phase displacement. Contrapuntal polyphony will necessarily be paired with contrapuntal polythythm, and so on. However, whilst the figures within this polyphony may perhaps be observing the rules of strict counterpoint, the figures of the polyrhythm could well be organised according to a free counterpoint; the situation is similar in the other categories: this is what I call phase-displacement. The category remains the same, even when its nature changes.

The value of the foregoing table may be questioned, since it only lists distinctions and has absolutely no generative power. In fact, this table is the starting point for the work of deduction: its general principles lead to the deployment of many different *appearances* of the sound phenomena. The particular case of heterophony will show how a large number of consequences, all generalisable, may be drawn from a single point of departure. This does not mean that heterophony assumes a specially important, or even exclusive role in the formulation of structures; it has been chosen as an example simply because, in the Western tradition, it has rarely been used even in an elementary state. (Beethoven used it for ornamental purposes—the Adagio of the Ninth Symphony—and in a certain number of slow movements of his other late works. Debussy used heterophonic figures with an acoustic aim—above all to 'construct' his orchestra: they appear more episodically in his later chamber works—the Sonata for flute, viola and harp, in particular. In any case, it has never really been considered as a structural principle, but now it seems indispensable as an intermediary stage between homophony and polyphony.)

There are two types of properties necessary for the formation of a heterophony: general properties which indicate the *placing*, and specific properties which result in the *production*. Exactly the same terms which were applied to the criteria of selection are used again here (fixity-mobility). Before entering into detail, heterophony must be precisely defined: it is a structural distribution of identical pitches, differentiated by divergent temporal co-ordinates, manifested by distinct intensities and timbres; as a result, the concept of heterophony will be extended from the monodic to the polyphonic level.

The general qualities necessary for the placing of heterophony are the following, going from the general to the particular:

1. *Nature*,
2. *Existence*,
3. *Number*,
4. *Dependence* (beginning or end of the heterophony).

Heterophony will be called convergent or divergent according to its degree of differentiation from the antecedent.

1. *Nature*: heterophony will be *ornamental*, when it brings inessential incidents into play; *structural*, when it obeys a true variation of structure, if not a structure altogether independent of the antecedent, and non-homogeneous with it.

2. *Existence*: heterophony will be *obligatory*, if, in every case, it must be played; *optional*, if there is the alternative of either omitting or playing it.

121

3. *Number:* heterophony will be single, double, triple, etc., according to whether one, two, three, etc., parallel structures are superimposed.

4. *Dependence:* heterophony will be *attached*, that is to say fixed to the antecedent, at an unchangeable determined point, whether it be a pitch (or a complex of pitches), or a rest; *floating*, when its departure or arrival takes place at a given interval of time—within a time field; this is bound to have repercussions on the writing, since the pitches must obey the difference of virtual phase depending on this time field.

Ex. 47

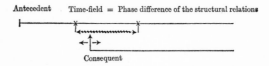

Thus, the placing of heterophony is defined by four general properties.

The specific properties which determine the mode of production will now be described. Here, the four properties of sound are brought into play:

a.1. *Absolute pitches*—the 'eidetically'[1] defined sounds;

a.2. *Relative pitches*—the sounds placed in actual registers;

b.1. *Duration-rhythms*—the static value of the durations, and of their relations;

b.2. *Tempo-rhythm*—the kinematic placing of these relations;

c.　*Timbre*—the instrument or group of instruments by means of which the heterophony is realised (non-instrumentally speaking, the relationship between formal characteristics and 'formants');

d.1. *General intensity*—the relationship of the external dynamic structures;

d.2. *Dynamic profile*—the evolution of the internal structures of amplitude.

[1] *Eidetical:* exhibiting likeness; of, relating to, having the character of essences, forms, images. (Trans.)

First, the *absolute pitches:* four possibilities are open to heterophony, according to whether the *transposition* on a given interval or intervals or the *multiplication by* a given interval or intervals is considered; this given interval can also be the unison. The interval or intervals on and by which the transpositions and multiplications are made can be fixed or mobile; in other words, in the course of a heterophony, whether connected or not with the internal structure of the antecedent, the interval of relation can change as often as necessary.

The following table applies to *absolute pitches:*

$$\begin{bmatrix} \text{without transposition/with transposition} \\ \text{(fixed/mobile)} \\ \text{(on one or more given intervals)} \\ \text{without multiplication/with multiplication} \\ \text{(fixed/mobile)} \\ \text{(by one or more given intervals)} \end{bmatrix}$$

We now come to *relative pitches,* in other words, the actual registers, fields of pitch in which the 'eidetic' sounds are placed. Heterophony can use a band of frequencies identical to that of the antecedent; that is to say, it can use the parallel frequencies in their entirety; but it can also be confined to reduced bands of frequencies, according to the principle of pass-band filters: thus, there may be one or several bands of varying widths.

The result takes the following forms:

$$\text{Bands of frequencies} \begin{bmatrix} \text{identical} \\ \text{reduced} \begin{cases} \text{several bands} \\ \text{a single band} \end{cases} \end{bmatrix}$$

An examination of duration-rhythms will show four methods of establishing relations with the antecedent:

1. A similar organisation, by simple or complex transformation, but always parallel to the original.

2. A dissimilar organisation, in which there will be no evolutionary relationship between the heterophony and the antecedent.

3. Transformation by identical values: the values of the heterophony are placed in an ambit identical to that of the antecedent.

4. Transformation by selected values: the principle of pass-band filters is applied to the durations.

These four relations are paired interchangeably as follows:

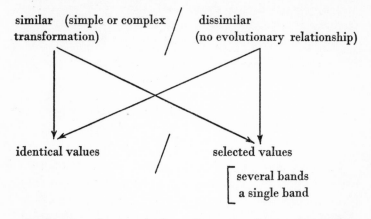

similar   (simple or complex   dissimilar
transformation)   (no evolutionary relationship)

identical values   selected values

several bands
a single band

In the case of *tempo-rhythms*, there are only two possibilities of production: either the tempo within the heterophony remains fixed, stable, or else the pace is mobile, involving acceleration and deceleration, combinations of the two and their conjunction with a stable speed. To summarise:

fixed/mobile (accleration–deceleration–combinations in
pairs and in groups of three).

We now come to *timbre*—that is, in the case of instrumental music, to the instrument or group of instruments; here there are also two possibilities, each subdivided into two categories.

On the one hand, the instrument or group of instruments allotted to the heterophony may remain invariable: in this case, it is either identical to that of the antecedent, or different; on the other hand, the instrument, or the group, may be variable: in this case it can change or evolve, either coincidentally with or independently of the other structures.

124

This can be shown in the following form:

$$\left[\text{invariable}\begin{cases}\text{identical}\\\text{different}\end{cases}\Big/\text{changing}\begin{cases}\text{with the other structures}\\\text{independently of the}\\\text{other structures}\end{cases}\right.$$

General intensity presents a similar situation. Intensities, or complexes of intensities, can be similar to those of the antecedent by simple or complex transformations—running parallel or anti-parallel; they can also be dissimilar, having no common structure. In addition, heterophony will be ordered either within a band of identical intensities, that is to say, in the same dynamic ambit, or in bands of intensity selected according to so-called filters of intensity.

These four possibilities are interchangeably paired and ordered, according to the following table:

$$\left[\begin{array}{l}\text{similar}\begin{cases}\text{parallel}\\\text{anti-parallel}\end{cases}\Big/\text{dissimilar}\\\text{band of identical intensities}\begin{cases}\text{selected}\\\text{intensities}\end{cases}\begin{cases}\text{a single band}\\\text{several bands}\end{cases}\end{array}\right.$$

As to the *dynamic profile*, it will be similar—parallel or anti-parallel—or dissimilar.

Finally, the filter-bands, especially those of intensity and duration, can also function by *extrapolation* from their original band.

A general table is given to facilitate the recognition and comparison of the various characteristics. This table is intended to show all the actions and interactions of which heterophony is capable.

HETEROPHONIC DETERMINATION

GENERAL PROPERTIES—PLACING

1. *Nature:* ornamental/structural
2. *Existence:* obligatory/optional
3. *Number:* single/double/triple, etc.
4. *Dependence:* attached/floating

SPECIFIC PROPERTIES—PRODUCTION

a.1. *Absolute pitches:*
without transposition/with transposition (fixed/mobile)
without multiplication/with multiplication (fixed/mobile)

a.2. *Relative pitches:*

identical/reduced bands of frequencies $\begin{cases} \text{a single band} \\ \text{several bands} \end{cases}$

b.1. *Duration-rhythm:* similar/dissimilar
identical/selected values

b.2 *Tempo-rhythm:* fixed/mobile

c. *Timbre:*

invariable $\begin{cases} \text{identical} \\ \text{different} \end{cases}$ / changing $\begin{cases} \text{with other structures} \\ \text{independently of} \\ \text{other structures} \end{cases}$

d.1. *General intensity:*

similar $\begin{cases} \text{parallel} \\ \text{anti-parallel} \end{cases}$ / dissimilar
band of identical intensities/band of selected intensities

d.2. *Dynamic profile:*

similar $\begin{cases} \text{parallel} \\ \text{anti-parallel} \end{cases}$ / dissimilar

N.B.—Heterophony will be convergent or divergent, according to the degree of differentiation from the antecedent.

The following examples have been delayed until now, in order to avoid continual interruption.

An original antecedent figure (Ex. 48a) is transformed in B by transposition or inversion, and the two form a homophony; the combination of A and B has figure C as its answering phrase. The latter observes exactly the same absolute and relative intervals, but follows a dissimilar rhythmic structure, with selected (and extrapolated) values; the tempo is fixed and identical, the instrumentation, intensity and dynamic profile are unchanged.

Ex. 48

In another example,

Ex. 49

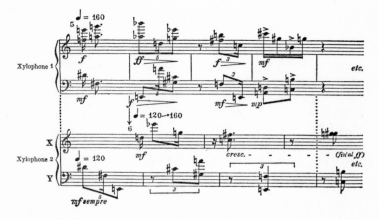

the tempo is mobile and the dynamics dissimilar within a
single band of intensities for the first heterophony (X); the
tempo is fixed, but different, the dynamics filtered to a single
band (mf) for the second (Y). In a third example, the sound
objects do not vary in themselves from the antecedent to the
heterophony, except in their arrangement.

127

Ex. 50

The first two cells A and B

Ex. 51

follow each other in the antecedent, while they are combined in
the heterophony; cell C is shared between the two organisations;
cell D is varied rhythmically and in dynamic profile, and its two
notes are presented simultaneously in the heterophony, whereas
they follow each other in the antecedent. With the help of these
three examples, it is easy to imagine the other cases mentioned
above; the pass-band filter is one of the most interesting, above
all when one is dealing with 'mutations' in the antecedent
original: the effect of 'truncation' is worth noting.

There is, of course, no hierarchy among these possibilities:
they can react upon each other, take reciprocal control of each
other, in short, enter into a compositional dialectic; any one
possesses a necessary but sufficient premise for taking on the
responsibility for any other. In fact, there is nothing to prevent
the definition of one characteristic by another; in Ex. 49, the
mobile tempo (accelerando) of the first heterophony is under-
lined by the parallelism of the dynamics (crescendo); the fixed

tempo of the second heterophony is in direct relationship with its fixed dynamics. When certain characteristics have a very precise structure, they can be 'blurred' by the superposition of other structures which do not coincide with them; a technique of 'fading' thus occurs, which will be invaluable in making link-passages more supple: blurred zones will occur, in which the form is caused to change direction.

Thus, an organised world is capable—without exterior intervention, or non-intrinsic activation—of assuring the coherence of the text, however far removed it may be from the fixed or determinate; nevertheless, indeterminacy or determinacy are produced in an ensemble of precisely established liaisons (as Rougier says, we must substitute the concept of coherence for the concept of evidence, the concept of tautology for that of necessity).

The resources of heterophony have been described at length; I could continue by demonstrating the possiblities of monody, polyphony or the double or triple concepts envisaged above, that is to say, heterophony of heterophonies, polyphony of polyphonies, etc. The important point is to distinguish clearly the two sorts of criteria which apply to every technique of development—*placing* and *production*. Placing is, to a certain extent, the exterior envelope which covers the existence, nature, density and dependence of the organisms; production is related to the actual generative processes, to the intrinsic characteristics of the structures. This double operation is of prime importance; its neglect leads to incomplete characterisation, to non-sense. A placing dependent on tempo, for example, demands that the evolution of the structures should conform to the variability of this tempo; similarly, structures defined by criteria of pitches demand a placing whose dependence will be rigorously circumscribed.

What then, finally, and more generally speaking, are the properties of a structure? The same distinction exists on this higher level: certain properties will be intrinsic, others extrinsic. The intrinsic properties apply globally to the functions of combination or arrangement, and to the functions of definition or selection. Under the heading of functions of combination, the different types of writing which make use of elementary concepts have been described: horizontal, vertical, diagonal, on the one hand, individual and collective on the other; under the heading of functions of definition the two fundamental categories were considered: fixity and variability, in other words, repose and movement. These two families of functions will determine the intrinsic *character* of every structure, seen from the most general point of view. The extrinsic properties are concerned with placing, that is to say, with the disposition of the structures in relation to each other, as well as their inter-relationship; these properties thus partly answer questions of simultaneity and homogeneity, partly those of dependence, independence or interdependence. We have already seen how form is the direct result of this manipulation of structures. The characterology of structures is in fact only the intrinsic property of a form which also has its own extrinsic properties. We will therefore return to this question in the following chapter.

A certain number of distinctions and classifications have already been established. These classifications should not be too rigidly adopted, their prime purpose having been the clarification of extreme possibilities. Their mechanical use will lead to absurdity and academicism; it would be far more useful to consider the combinations which can apply to simple cases, and the transitions which can be effected from one to the other. A certain quality of 'illusion', of 'porosity', can be developed from these general, sometimes schematic, considerations. This is why it would be wrong to believe that monody, heterophony and polyphony are stringently separate; it would be just as vain to oppose them at all costs, as it would be to neglect the deliberate use of their contradictions. Perhaps it was premature to announce that the use of a system of *part-writing* was no longer valid. Certainly, in the traditional sense, this mode of writing has become obsolete; it has justly been said that Webern, in each of his canonic parts, multiplies the accidents which serve to break its continuity: numerous changes of register, which bring about the crossing of the voices, frequent interruptions of phrases by rests, which greatly weaken the

130

perception of the phrase as a unitary phenomenon, continual use of *Klangfarbenmelodie*—each note, or each group of two notes often being given a new timbre. In short the figures are reduced to an extremely limited number of sounds, the predominance of certain intervals creating ambiguities which are impossible to disentangle. So much is true: it is equally true that Webern's scholasticism, adjusting the series to suit Flemish contrapuntal technique, allowed him to pass from an organisation of anarchic intervals to a determinate hierarchy. In my opinion, we have been too ready to equate a *non-homogeneity* of parts with a renunciation of one of the richest principles of Western music: two or more 'phenomena', evolving independently, but being constantly responsible to one another. Thus, we should aim at a transformation of the concept of *parts*, and not at its abolition, which annihilates one of the most important domains of the dialectic of composition. As a result of this lack, we see the frequent appearances, not of '-phonies' of a new kind, but of what might be called 'analysed objects' dependent on a certain structural 'cantus firmus' (I would be tempted to write: 'quantum firmum' . . .), one of the most disappointing regressions of the present time. This amounts to the embellishment of certain fundamental schemes with various combinations of sounds, a succession of *states* from which any fundamental dialectic is excluded. The stringing together of these structures finds its equivalent in their composition; if, for example, a band of frequencies is analysed by successions of durations, one can only obtain a simple 'filling-in', equivalent to the classical arpeggio. Changing the name of these 'worked' arpeggios will hardly be enough to transmute their deliberately poor and boring substance: astonishing stylistic lapses result—Bartókian chromatic flurries, Ravelian motley. The renunciation of *parts* that results in rather primary colouring reminds us that music is not a 'playing card', to adapt Cézanne's remark on painting; that 'depth', 'perspective', 'relief' have an important part to play. As asserted above, it would be vain to try to reinstate contrapuntal and harmonic writing: these died with Webern. The concepts of *parts* should be radically reconsidered; a

131

part will henceforth be considered as a constellation of events obeying a certain number of common criteria, a distribution in mobile and discontinuous time, respecting variable density, and using non-homogeneous timbre, of families of structures in evolution. These constellations and distributions will be responsible one to another, especially where pitch and duration are concerned; a constant control—such as complementary chromaticism and logarithmic relationships—will take account of the responsibility of the pitches amongst themselves; the control of the durations will extend to the field within which the pitches are related to each other. Dynamics and timbre will introduce the necessary flexibility. Without this rigorous control, an inorganic simultaneity of events will tend to occur. Moreover it should be remembered that complexity is not a question of density, even if these two concepts do happen to overlap; in any case, complexity, like density, must be ruled by technical and stylistic principles which will be expounded later.

An extension of the concept of *parts* will enable such categories as monody, heterophony and polyphony to be made 'porous'. We have already stressed the cardinal fact that the series dilutes the opposition between horizontal and vertical, just as it creates a universe where consonance and dissonance are abolished. Schoenberg's solution, however, remains far wide of the mark, because it is applied to an idea as out of date as the harmonisation of a theme. The most systematic examples (Fourth String Quartet, Piano Concerto, Violin Concerto) are forbidding enough, without mentioning the academic rhythm which is woven through them. These themes, whose cells are harmonised by complementary cells included in the series, are profoundly unsatisfying, however one may invoke the shade of Swedenborg or recite to oneself the Cubist conception of the object. On the one hand, there is no truly *harmonic* function binding the theme to its accompaniment: it is a question of pure chromatic complementarity; on the other hand, instead of merging the two dimensions, this usage contrasts them artificially. Webern is hardly more convincing when he uses this procedure (the first variation of the *Variations*, Opus 30) although the stylistic discrepancy is much less violent, mainly as a result of intervals that are disjunct in time and in space (rhythm and register having no academic associations in this case). This relativity of dimensions will thus not be realised in an 'inherited' form, even one that has been passed through the mill of the series. Again, Webern clearly shows the way ahead, especially in his choral works; his outlook becomes progressively more specific from Opus 19, through *Das Augenlicht* and the *First Cantata* to the *Second Cantata*. In the *Second Cantata*, these relationships have reached a completely explicit state: the following is a simple example from the third movement.

Ex. 52

The antecedent is given to the soprano solo, and is horizontally exposed; the three consequents divide the phrase into two parts, a and b, verticalising the first (a) and leaving the second in its original horizontal form (b). Aurally, the distance of the canonic entry (a dotted crotchet) is stressed to the utmost by this verticalisation, which 'schematises' the time, the same chord being transposed three times. A much more subtle example occurs in the fifth movement.

The four parts are first superposed at A, the zero time of the canon, in which the verticalisation contains the germ of the following horizontalisation; the vertical dimension is the result of the coincidence of several horizontal dimensions. In B, there is a horizontal canonic form, by diminution, in the tenor

133

Ex. 53

and bass parts; the third part, the alto, condenses the canonic figure half vertically, half horizontally. This figure is difficult to distinguish since certain of its notes are *virtual*, and have a more explicit meaning in another part (the A flat, by belonging to the violin solo, and to the rhythmic figure of the tenor part, cannot be considered as being *primarily* part of the alto). In C, there is a dissolution and a total *submergence* of the canon (I use this word deliberately as though speaking of the submergence of a subterranean river); the figures are compressed and borrow sounds from each other, to the point of losing all characteristic physiognomy, a loss which the instrumentation corroborates by confining all the figures to timbres of a similar nature. Only at the end of the tenor part do we find three notes in exact canon with the soprano; these notes, by their precision, serve to reintroduce the choir in the zero time of superposition. This second example is very characteristic in the flexibility of its transition from one dimension to the other; this time, there is no stylistic discrepancy, no point of internal contradiction: distributions simply change direction.

In this connection, attention must be drawn to the terms actual and virtual: here, these terms are applied to elementary objects, but their importance is seen when it is a question of making structures 'vanish', of removing all precise delimitation, or making them 'pivot', between two levels. To return to my definition: an object is generally virtual in a given structure when this structure has a lesser pregnance[1] than others in which the object also appears; the object is actual in the structure having the greatest pregnance. If this concept is widened to include ensembles, the virtual or actual structures will be defined according to the pregnance of the ensemble. In the interrelations of structures having objects in common, suppleness and complexity will largely arise from this concept; it is essential to the structural ambiguity mentioned earlier.

This ambiguity applies to the transition from one category to another; but it can give rise to static illusions, where polyphony, for example, can take on the aspect of homophony, even of monody, by a sort of *projection* of these elements onto an even plane. We will analyse some examples to clarify this idea.

Take four rhythmic values depending on the simple proportion: 1 2 3 4; the four different orders of succession will be: 1 3 2 4; 3 2 1 4; 1 4 3 2; 1 2 3 4. These four orders are multiplied respectively by the different terms of the same proportion, in the order: 4 2 3 1. Thus, four groups of durations are obtained, which, if the crotchet is taken as the unitary value, will observe the general proportion: 4 12 8 16; 6 4 2 8; 3 12 9 6; 1 2 3 4. (See Ex. 54)

These four groups are superposed in the horizontal dimension, observing the distances 1–2–2 as their linking principle:

[1] See p. 47.

Ex. 54

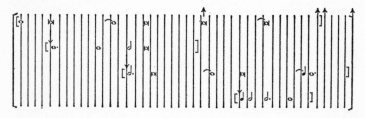

the second group will enter after *one* duration expressed by the first group, the third, after *two* durations expressed by the second, and the fourth, after *two* durations expressed by the third. The plan of this superposition is shown in Ex. 55a.

Ex. 55a

But, instead of exposing this superposition polyphonically, it is reduced to a single part; if the most recent part to enter is always exposed, the beginnings and ends of the parts not directly expressed will be indicated by grace notes. These parts will, as it were, *eclipse* each other; at certain moments, they will be actual, at others, virtual.

Ex. 55b

136

There is no need for a detailed account of the pitches, dynamics and timbres to which each organisation of time corresponds; a transcription of the raw sound material will be enough.

Ex. 56]

This material is formed from homophonies which are different in their constitution, density and disposition. This example thus shows a false homophony, which is really the *reduction* of a polyphony. In the use of dynamics and timbre, or register, an appearing and reappearing object can be considered as non-evolving, that is to say, it has an absolutely fixed form; but it can also be thought of as evolving subterraneously: subjacent curves will arise, whose intersections will obviate presentation of the object in a constant light.

A homophony was quoted above; a monodic example based on the same ambiguity follows: it is the static reduction of a polyphony which remains latent.

Ex. 57

I will not analyse it, because it is easily recognisable as having the same theoretical point of departure as the preceding example. Looking at these two examples, it can be clearly understood how, starting from an extreme rigidity of conception —of practically canonic writing—a suppleness of realisation is reached which can easily be mistaken for a flexible improvisation. The effect of a simple succession is totally excluded by irregular recurrences which fundamentally alter the perception of the canonic form itself.

In the next example, homophony takes on the appearance of polyphony.

Ex. 58

Suppose that a given monody is split up according to its recurring pitches; the note D♮ occurs four times (a1, a2, a3, a4), C♮ twice (b1, b2), etc. By a local procedure, a description of whose method would be irrelevant in this context, we can attach all the D's to a single organisation, all the C's to a derived organisation, etc. Example 59 shows an organisation of variable density.

Ex. 59

Example 60 shows how each D of the monody is simultaneously commented upon by purely vertical objects, whose duration is prolonged until the end of the phrase marked by the last D. For each pitch, imagine similar complementary organisms, or commentaries, each one being horizontally disposed, and strictly limited to the duration of the pitch in the monody, etc. The entanglement of all the successive commentaries will create an impression of polyphony, contradicted, however, by their invariable coincidence with the features of the monody. This ambiguity of perception will be increased when the monody, explicit in this example, is suppressed: it will only appear in the general structure in a virtual state.

138

Ex. 60

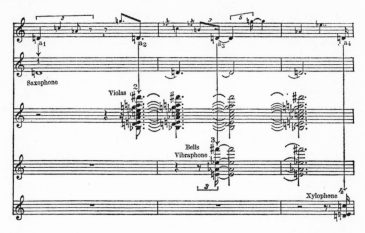

Combinations of these different states have already appeared in previous examples, so now it will be enough to specify them. Taking Ex. 48, the original A is amplified by a homophony B; consequently the heterophony C is built upon a homophony. Likewise, in the last example, the monody is the reduction of a polyphony—which explains the recurrence and the extremely limited selection of pitches; Ex. 60 apparently shows a polyphony grafted on to a monody: in reality it is a homophony which has been deduced from a combination of perspectives from which each draws a new individuality. Seen from this point of view, the concepts of 'vertical', 'horizontal', 'parts' and 'chords' are no longer clear cut, their edges are 'frayed' and their possibilities multiplied ten-fold. This creates a technique of development no less solidly based than the old, but no longer needing to bend out-of-date means to renovatory ends.

A last question arises in connection with the modes of linking the various structures, whether of the same or of different types; there are both end-to-end links and 'lap-joints', in which the end of one structure overlaps the beginning of another. The control of the structures will be purely local if they always observe the same mode of linking, that is to say, when they are fixed in place once and for all and are linked at both ends to other fixed structures. It will be quite different in the case of mobile structures, where one is dealing with the interlinking of entire families of elements. It is often said that the relationships between mobile organisations are impossible to foresee in their entirety and that it would therefore be presumptuous to claim *foreknowledge* of their linking potential. Most of the works based on mobile structures do indeed show little concern for this important question and the resulting links are sometimes good, sometimes bad, according to the hazard of encounters that could hardly be more . . . hazardous. Considering the problem seriously, there is no doubt that, if they fulfil certain conditions, families of structures can be linked to others without each of the links needing to be precisely controlled. One has only to select a general criterion of linking which will eliminate all others. Let us briefly look at this method. The control operating within the structure itself will not need to act on the linking as well. To understand this, we must refer to the two definitions of pitch: absolute and relative pitch. Suppose that a family of structures A is to be linked to a family B; if the absolute pitches used at the end of A are quite different from those of B, no linking can fail to be satisfactory since the terminal zone of each A will necessarily be complementary to the initial zone of each B. This can be achieved quite simply by the use of defective series: the A structures will be based on defective series of a certain category, the B structures on defective series of a complementary category.

Although series of absolute pitches do not obey any particular law, care should be taken that at the moment of linking the relative pitches are fixed in a certain, immovable disposition of registers. *Nodes* of register will be obtained in the area of structural linking, whereas *antinodes* of register will separate these within the structures. Hence, mixed organisations of absolute and relative pitches may freely be created. If structure A makes use of a defective series having a certain number of notes in common with the defective series which characterises B, the common notes should have a fixed register, so as to create a partial *node* in the tessitura; the other notes are in no

140

way tied down by this necessity, and may be disposed in any register. Thus structures A and B are controlled from within, and their joins cannot be other than satisfactory.

Apart from this possibility, contrasted placing, based on differences of pregnance and of style, facilitates the work of external control. To link a family A ending in 'blocks' to a family B beginning with 'blocks', is a relatively easy task: the compositional precautions are minimal, in view of the pregnance of each block; it is simply a matter of checking the extreme registers of each initial or final block. Taking the same precaution, a family A ending in 'points' can be linked to a family B commencing with 'blocks', and vice versa. To summarise, the difference in pregnance of the structures with regard to their constituents will create a divergence of attraction sufficiently strong to validate their linking.

But structures of identical pregnance can be conceived independently of one another; in which case, control will be exercised from 'individuality' to 'individuality'; hence, adjustments will be necessary for the cohesion of the linking.

These different methods apply, of course, both to the simultaneities of structures and to shifts carried out on the superpositions. In order that one structure may be superposed on another, it must now be entirely subject to the rules given above; when planning a shift of structures, these rules must be respected for the field of time in which the shifting of the superposition is to be produced.

Equal care should be taken with the use of variable tempo on a given structure. Certain elementary data sometimes seem to have been disregarded, to a point where procedures, in themselves good, have seemed bad, solely as a result of their defective application. In fact, tempo variation alters the significance of structures, sometimes considerably; structures are put to the test by tempo in something like the way that models in a wind-tunnel are tested in air currents of great velocity. They are deformed, they undergo torsions of every sort, they resist—or do not resist! Beyond certain limits, internal structural relationships are radically upset; speed forbids any detailed articulation and warps the structure by compressing it (always supposing that it is still playable); slowness causes the collapse of articulation, and distends or dislocates the structure. A structure having subtly differentiated durations cannot be subjected to a rapid tempo; conversely, a structure whose values are analysed by a unit of subdivision cannot sustain a slow tempo: beyond the analytical unit, the metrical value cannot be reconstituted, for this regular analytical unit will itself be taken as the metrical value. In structures which are only suited to an established tempo, the only possible modifications of this basic tempo are those capable of changing the *slope* of a structure, but unable to alter its direction and sense. Structures using a limited number of differentiated durations, where these move and are renewed within a moderate ambit, can sustain extreme transformations of tempo; here, the ratio between the extreme tempi will—by inverse proportion—give an idea of the ratio between the extreme durations (incidentally, the same goes for dynamics).

PROVISORY CONCLUSION

We end our investigation of technique itself on the threshold of form. We have proceeded from the definition of the series to its description and its use; then we studied the sound world to which serial functions are applied; in short, we sketched out a morphology. From there, we passed to the outline of a syntax, studying the extrinsic and intrinsic characterology of structures. All the same, it must be remembered that the real work of *composition* begins here, at a point where it is often thought that only applications have still to be discovered; all these methods must be given a *meaning*.

Therefore, let us not underestimate the implications of the studies we have undertaken; these should not be regarded as a set of recipes, a basis for 'manufacture'. I proceeded from the elementary to the most general level in order to stress that this was not a catalogue of more or less useful procedures, but an attempt to construct a coherent system by means of a methodical investigation of the musical world, deducing multiple consequences from a certain number of rational points of departure. I consider that methodical investigation and the search for a coherent system are an indispensable basis for all creation, more so than the actual attainments which are the source or the consequence of this investigation. I hope it will not be said that such a step leads to aridity, that it kills all fantasy, and, since it is difficult to avoid the fateful word, all inspiration. Far from seeing the pursuit of a method and the establishment of a system as proof of a withering of the faculties, I see it on the contrary, as containing the most powerful form of invention, wherein the imagination plays an essential, determining role. This is certainly not an original thought on my part, for the claim that intelligence must participate in elaboration was formulated long ago in the field of poetry. Baudelaire overcame this opposition between 'lucidity' and 'genius' a century ago, and in what terms! Creation, according to him, had to be directed by an intellectual appreciation of poetry: 'I pity the poets,' he wrote, 'who are guided only by instinct; I believe them to be incomplete . . . Somewhere in every poet there must be a critic.' It is high time to adopt this attitude in music. 'Technique' is not, in fact, a dead weight to be dragged around as a guarantee of immortality. It is an exalting mirror which the imagination forges for itself, and in which its discoveries are reflected; the imagination cannot, without running the risk of weakness, rely on 'instinct' alone, as Baudelaire emphasises. Over-reliance on this instinct has led it, like the cuckoo, to lay its eggs in the nests of others. Imagination must stimulate intelligence and intelligence must anchor imagination: without this reciprocal action, any investigation is likely to be chimerical. This is why, before approaching form, we have attempted a synthesis of present-day technique, in order to be able to act in good conscience, and with freedom: far from being a dead weight, this equipment will serve as a viaticum and *provoke* us to speculation. It has often been said that music is as much a science as an art; how could these two entities be fired in the same crucible, except by the Imagination, that 'queen of faculties'!

143

INDEX

Aragon, 23–4

Bartók, 131
Baudelaire, 11–12, 15, 18–19, 143
Beethoven: Sonata in C minor, Op.
    13, 50
  Symphony No. 9 in D minor, Op.
    125, 121
Berg, 100–1, 103, 105
  Lulu, 101
  Lyric Suite, 71–3, 77–8, 101
  Wozzeck, 61, 100
Berlioz, 66
  Requiem, 67
Boulez: *Pli selon pli* (*Tombeau*), 64
  Poésie pour pouvoir, 68
  Third Piano Sonata (*Trope*), 73–6,
    79
Breton, 23
Brillouin, 31
Butor, 18–19

Cézanne, 131
'Croche, Monsieur', *see* Debussy
Cubism, 132

Dada, 16, 24
Debussy, 13–15, 34
  Sonata for flute, viola and harp,
    121

Fokker, 89

Guilleaume, 32fn

Huyghens, 90

Jarry, 24, 29fn

Lévi-Strauss, 32
Lichtenberg, 24

Miller, 20

Nietzsche, 24

Pascal, 13, 25
Pasch, 30

Rameau, 31
Ravel, 131
Rimbaud, 25
Rougier, 30–2, 83, 129

Schaeffer, 66fn
Schoenberg, 100–1, 103, 132
Stravinsky: *Les Noces*, 50
Swedenborg, 132

Vaché, 23

Weber-Fechner, 102
Webern, 19, 100–1, 103, 105, 130–1,
    132–5
  Concerto, Op. 24, 71, 77–8
  Das Augenlicht, Op. 24, 133
  First Cantata, Op. 29, 133
  Quartet, Op. 28, 71, 81
  Second Cantata, Op. 31, 46, 100,
    133–5
  Two Songs, Op. 19, 133
  Variations, Op. 30, 132

144